Student Handbook to Sociology

Social Change

Volume VII

Student Handbook to Sociology

Social Change

Volume VII

MIKAILA MARIEL LEMONIK ARTHUR

Liz Grauerholz
General Editor

Facts On File
An Infobase Learning Company

Student Handbook to Sociology: Social Change
Copyright © 2012 Mikaila Mariel Lemonik Arthur

Facts On File, Inc.
An Imprint of Infobase Learning
132 West 31st Street
New York NY 10001

Library of Congress Cataloging-in-Publication Data

Student handbook to sociology/Liz Grauerholz, general editor.
　　v. cm.
　　Includes bibliographical references and index.
　　Contents: v. 1. Histories and theories—v. 2. Research methods—v. 3. Social structure—v. 4. Socialization—v. 5. Stratification and inequality—v. 6. Deviance and crime—v. 7. Social change.
　　ISBN 978-0-8160-8314-5 (alk. paper)—ISBN 978-0-8160-8315-2 (v. 1 : alk. paper)—ISBN 978-0-8160-8316-9 (v. 2 : alk. paper)—ISBN 978-0-8160-8317-6 (v. 3 : alk. paper)—ISBN 978-0-8160-8319-0 (v. 4 : alk. paper)—ISBN 978-0-8160-8320-6 (v. 5 : alk. paper)—ISBN 978-0-8160-8321-3 (v. 6 : alk. paper)—ISBN 978-0-8160-8322-0 (v. 7 : alk. paper) 1. Sociology. I. Grauerholz, Elizabeth, 1958-
　　HM585.S796 2012　　301—dc23　　　　　　2011025983

Text design by Erika K. Arroyo
Composition by Kerry Casey
Cover printed by Yurchak Printing, Landisville, Pa.
Book printed and bound by Yurchak Printing, Landisville, Pa.
Date Printed: April 2012
Printed in the United States of America

10 9 8 7 6 5 4 3 2 1

T 17612

CONTENTS

ACKNOWLEDGMENTS

Thanks first of all to Liz Grauerholz, who invited me to work on this project. My parents, Baila Lemonik and Dwight Arthur, have given me a life-long focus on how social change is created. Benjamin Ledsham provided essential support throughout the writing process. Many of the ideas on these pages were first tested out in my Social Change and Social Movements course at Queens College of the City University of New York in 2006. Introduction to sociology courses, courses in the sociology of the Holocaust, and courses in law and society at New York University, Queens College, Hamilton College, and Rhode Island College have also helped me refine and polish these ideas. I especially want to acknowledge the role of my students in making this text a reality. It is these students who have taught me how to explain things—and who continue to make it all worthwhile.

FOREWORD

In this volume on social change, the author introduces you to one of the most interesting and time-tested subjects in sociology. In fact, if you trace sociology back to its roots (to the founding mothers and fathers), you will find that it was social change that compelled scholars to try to understand and explain social life. Throughout the 20th century, much of this interest focused on industrialization and modernization and their impact on society at large. Contemporary sociologists also recognize that understanding societies and social groups means taking into account social change: why and how it occurs, as well as its impact on society and individuals.

By now you've probably learned that a fundamental sociological "truth" is that social life is predictable. Sociologists are able to study what they study because people and groups behave in patterned ways. Given this, the idea of "social change" would seem outside the purview of sociology because change implies unpredictability. As you will see, however, the subject of social change is at the heart of sociology; in fact, you will learn that even social change is patterned and to some degree predictable.

Consider for a moment something that appears to be chaotic and completely devoid of social norms—panic situations. Many people believe that panic situations create a "everyone for himself" mentality and that social norms cease to exist, not so much because people are inherently selfish but because they do not know how to define the situation and therefore cannot easily determine which social norms should apply. When 11 concert-goers were killed at a The Who concert in 1979, for example, most attributed the tragedy to "mob psychology." The consensus was that everyone acted in selfish, ruthless ways, interested only in saving themselves. The reality, as sociologist Norris Johnson learned, was quite different. By interviewing concert-goers and police who were at the event,

Johnson found that participants did try to help each other, sometimes risking their own safety to do so. Johnson's findings are evidence that norms govern even the most chaotic situations and that something as seemingly random as mob behavior (what sociologists call collective behavior) is patterned and can be studied and explained. In this volume you will see how such behaviors are linked to social change, how and why social change occurs, and the many ways that it is patterned and ordered.

Social change is a feature of all societies and has existed across all historical periods. There is no question, however, that contemporary society is characterized by exceptionally rapid and widespread social change. Many of us feel powerless in the face of such sweeping change and struggle to keep up with all that's going on around us. Some of us long for a roadmap or instructions on how to cope with all of the chaos. This volume may provide a bit of both as it invites you to look forward and to consider your own role in social change. And herein lies one of the most important sociological lessons: Although we are constantly affected by the social world, we also affect and shape that social world. By understanding the social forces at work in our lives, we become better informed and better able to embrace those changes that enhance our lives and even to resist those that don't. In this way, the sociological perspective can help each of us be, as Mahatma Gandhi suggested, "the change you want to see in the world."

—Liz Grauerholz, University of Central Florida

INTRODUCTION

The world today is a very different place than it was when your parents were your age—and an even more different place than it was just 100 years ago. The study of these differences is the study of social change, and it is essential to understanding who we are, where we came from, and where we are going. Sometimes, social change occurs suddenly, as when an environmental catastrophe or a political revolution changes the course of history. Sometimes, it occurs gradually as lots of people individually make decisions about where to live, how many children to have, and what technologies to use, and all of these decisions build a different world. Social change can happen because of impersonal forces like the environment, because one individual makes a striking new discovery, or because a large group of people get together with the goal of creating change. This book will consider all of these various pathways that social change has taken; it will also look at forces that propel social change and at ways people themselves can contribute to social change.

The survey of social change in this book has been designed to accomplish two goals. First, it has been designed to introduce readers to the phenomena of social change so that they can understand how our world got to be the way it is today and how change will continue to work in ways that will shape their lives. Second, it has been designed to give readers an introduction to the tools necessary for creating social change themselves. It thus considers a variety of specific types of social change, as well as the factors that produce social change, the consequences of change, and how we can and do respond to social change. Chapter 2 considers population change, looking at how populations grow and how they shrink. It then explores the dynamics of environmental change and how changes in the environment can be produced by—and subsequently affect—human societies. The chapter also examines the growth of cities and suburbs.

Chapter 3 discusses technological change, beginning with the Industrial Revolution and the emergence of capitalism and bureaucracy and continuing with an overview of the contemporary period, with a focus on the development of the knowledge economy and advanced technology. Chapter 4 explores the development globalization and modernity.

Although all forms of social change are produced by human societies, some admit a more direct role for groups of people who are actively seeking to make something happen. Chapter 5 considers collective behavior, the term for actions taken by groups of people working together. Collective behavior includes phenomena such as mobs, riots, fads, manias, panics, social movements, and revolutions. Chapter 5 explores all of these except for the final two, which are the focus of Chapters 6 and 7, respectively. Chapter 6 outlines how social movements emerge, what they do, and how social movements enable groups of people to make an impact on the world—thus producing social change. Other types of change-oriented collective action are explored in Chapter 7. This chapter begins with a discussion about how elite segments of society work to create—or prevent—social change. It then examines revolutions that aim to fundamentally reshape governments and societies. Finally, it focuses on terrorism. The last chapter in the book discusses ways in which ordinary people can respond to social change, presenting opportunities for readers to see how they themselves fit within the broader story.

CHAPTER 1

WHAT IS SOCIAL CHANGE?

The discipline of sociology was born at a time of massive transformation: the Industrial Revolution, the rise of democracy and of communism, and the emergence of wars that spanned the globe. Thus, understanding why and how such transformations occur was one of the first and has remained one of the most enduring interests of sociologists. We call such transformations, whether they occur in politics, technology, or any other area of social life, **social change**. The study of social change brings with it a wide range of questions: why—and when—does social change occur? What are the varieties of social change, and how do they differ from one another? What processes make social change possible? How can individuals or groups contribute to creating social change? And what, if anything, can be done to halt social change? To begin answering these questions, consider the story of Carrie Buck.

Carrie Buck was born in Virginia in 1906. Her mother Emma, a poor woman who worked as a prostitute and who may have been an alcoholic, was abandoned by Carrie's father, and Carrie was placed in foster care soon after her birth. Though she went to school until sixth grade, foster children at the time were often treated more as domestic servants than as children, and that seems to have been Carrie's fate as well. When Carrie was 17, she was raped by her foster parents' nephew and became pregnant, and in 1924 she was committed to the Virginia Colony for the Epileptic and Feeble-Minded (where her mother was already a resident) on the grounds of being feebleminded, poorly behaved, and sexually promiscuous ("feebleminded" used to be considered a fairly precise scientific term to discuss those with learning or developmental disabilities). Carrie's foster parents took on the care of her daughter, Vivian.

Right around the same time that Carrie was committed to the Virginia Colony, the Commonwealth of Virginia passed the Racial Integrity Act of 1924, a law that permitted those with intellectual or psychological disabilities and those with epilepsy to be sterilized against their will—and indeed without their knowledge. Carrie would be a test case for the new law. In order to ensure that there would be no legal obstacles to this course of action, the state initiated a court case that went all the way to the United States Supreme Court. A legal guardian was appointed to defend Carrie's interests, but the guardianship was essentially in name only as both sides were really working together to make sure the case maintained the legality of sterilization. Indeed it did. In 1927, the Supreme Court issued its decision in *Buck v. Bell*, stating that compulsory sterilization was indeed legal, and that "three generations of imbeciles is enough."

Carrie was sterilized. Shortly afterward, she was released from the Virginia Colony—her supposed feeblemindedness being considered a problem only if she were to bear children. She was married for twenty-five years until her husband died; her daughter Vivian died of an intestinal disease at age eight. Before her own death in 1983, Carrie told a researcher she was sad to have not been able to bear additional children. Incidentally, there is no evidence that either Carrie or Vivian was feebleminded—on the contrary, Vivian earned Bs and Cs in school.

Despite what happened to Carrie, she might have been lucky compared to other people who were seen as disabled in the 1920s. Though war veterans who became disabled in combat were given access to certain rehabilitative services, many people with disabilities—whether developmental, psychological, or physical—were simply placed in institutions. Depending on their condition, they were confined, ignored, or subject to treatments like lobotomies (procedures in which part of the brain is destroyed). Many never had contact with family and were denied an education; by 1945, children as young as five were routinely being placed in such institutions.

Even people with disabilities who were able to continue living at home with their families could not expect to have a good quality of life. For most of the 20th century, even as public education became mandatory, few schools would accommodate children with disabilities. Before 1975, only 20 percent of children with disabilities were enrolled in public schools; indeed, many states prohibited blind or deaf children, children with emotional difficulties, and children with learning disabilities from attending school. Children with comparatively mild disabilities might have been accepted into schools, but there were no special provisions (such as extra time on tests, desks that would accommodate a wheelchair, or someone to read test questions out loud) to make the classroom environment user friendly for such children. Those who struggled usually dropped out.

Even those who did finish school were likely to have trouble getting jobs—in large part because of the stigma surrounding disability. In 1962, for instance, a survey conducted by the Minnesota Department of Public Welfare found that 40 percent of the people surveyed believed those with mental retardation were also mentally ill, 35 percent believed they should be kept in institutions, 24 percent believed they would make poor employees, and 23 percent believed they should not play in public playgrounds. People had similar opinions about people with other sorts of disabilities, often believing that those who were blind or deaf, had epilepsy, or had mobility impairments were unable to think, speak, or contribute. In such an environment it is perhaps not surprising that President Franklin D. Roosevelt, who had suffered from polio as a child and thus used wheelchair, worked hard to conceal this fact from the voting public. Though these stigmas have diminished somewhat, they still remain a fact of life for people with disabilities. A 2010 Roper Poll found that 51 percent of people believe that those with learning disabilities are really just lazy and over 45 percent believe that blindness or deafness is associated with learning disabilities. As a consequence, people with disabilities remain disproportionately likely to be unemployed, even in our supposedly more enlightened society.

But concrete changes did occur during the decades between Roosevelt's decision to conceal his need for a wheelchair and the Roper Poll's more recent findings. In the late 1960s, people with disabilities began to demand equal rights and equal treatment in American society, just as women, people of color, gay and lesbian people, and other groups were doing. They held protests, lobbied elected officials, and created cooperative living environments to show the world that they could and would live the way they wanted to. In 1977, activists even held sit-ins in Federal Health, Education, and Welfare offices around the country. Technology played a role in these initial changes and has become increasingly more important. Advances like the hearing aid, text messaging, voice recognition software, text-to-speech conversion, and power wheelchairs have made it much more possible for people who have disabilities to fully participate in education, employment, and almost every other aspect of life.

In 1975, the United States Congress passed the Individuals with Disabilities Education Act (IDEA), a law requiring that public schools accommodate children with disabilities by providing an education adapted to their needs. And in 1990, Congress passed the Americans with Disabilities Act (ADA), prohibiting public facilities, commuter transportation (not airlines), commercial facilities, and most (not all) employers from discriminating against persons with disabilities. Today, people with disabilities who are capable of making decisions for themselves generally cannot be confined to medical or residential facilities against their will. They must be provided with an adequate education. And as long as they can perform job functions in environments with reasonable accommodations, they cannot be fired from their jobs or discriminated against when applying for jobs. Despite the continuing inequalities that people with disabilities face, this is a remarkable difference—one that activists fought for. How did it happen?

DEFINING SOCIAL CHANGE

Ask a group of people what they think of when they hear the phrase "social change" and you are likely to get as many answers as there are people in the group: from welfare reform to independence movements, from acceptance of

What Do You Think of When You Think of Social Change?

Close your eyes for a moment and consider what the term social change means to you. Is it the fall of the Berlin Wall and the end of the Cold War? The American Revolution? The invention of the computer? The Internet? The Civil Rights Movement?

marriage for same-sex couples to the fair trade movement, from the development of the Internet to fighting back against change. These are all indeed examples of social change. So what, then, does this simple phrase that encompasses so very many things actually mean?

Social change can be defined as encompassing all kinds of changes in the social, political, or economic structures of society. Because almost anything can affect social, political, and economic structures, almost any change that we can observe in the world can be a social change. In some cases, changes

Fill in your own images of social change—and keep them in mind as you read this book.

(clockwise, on opposite page)
Crowd around the Berlin Wall on November 9, 1989. *(Sue Ream. Wikipedia)*; **Soldiers from Delaware and Maryland regiments are represented holding off the British during the fierce battle at Brooklyn Heights on August 27, 1776. Although the British eventually prevailed, this action allowed Washington to withdraw his forces to Long Island in an orderly fashion.** *(National Guard)*; **IBM personal computer.** *(Marcin Wichary. Wikipedia)*; **Civil rights march on Washington, D.C.** *(Library of Congress)*

are obviously social in nature. One example of this is the move from extended family groups living in small villages to nuclear family groups (or even solitary individuals) living in large metropolitan areas. But even those changes which are not obviously social in nature can have significant consequences for social life. Changes in religious belief systems, changes in economic productivity, and even changes in the Earth's physical environment all shape and alter social life. Consider changes in the environment. If an area that had been getting a significant amount of rainfall each year experiences a drought, society will have to change to respond to new environmental conditions. The people affected by the drought might move to another area; they might have to change the kinds of crops they grow or develop new irrigation technologies; hygiene practices might have to change; and even recreational activities might have to change (people accustomed to swimming in the river may turn to sports and other activities that can be practiced on dry land). Other specific examples that show the diverse nature of social change include changes in a society's political structure, economic system, social structure, and cultural structure.

The term **political structure** refers to the networks of relationships between groups and institutions within the political sphere, including governments, political parties, and interest groups; to norms governing political behavior, including laws and regulations; and to the organization of power and influence in society. Given the number of possible variables, changes in political structure can be rather multifaceted. For instance, the balance of power between different sectors of society—businesses versus government or the rich versus the poor—can change. New alliances between groups or new factions within groups can emerge, as can new political ideologies and identities, thus changing political dynamics. One example of how this complex shift works is the Tea Party movement that emerged in 2009, which changed the campaign strategies and platforms of numerous political candidates and also mobilized people who had not previously been active in politics, thus influencing election outcomes in various parts of the country.

Legal changes also spark changes within the political structure. Consider, for example, what can occur when rules regulating campaign financing are relaxed. Lifting (or failing to enforce) such rules can allow wealthy corporations to donate more money to political candidates, and the post-election influence of such wealthy corporate donors may increase proportionately. Thus, it is not just a matter of which laws are passed; enforcement of these laws, as well as other law enforcement actions and governmental repression, can also alter the dynamics of the political structure. In the United States, for example, criminal penalties for illegal drug use increased substantially in the 1980s. So did related law enforcement activities. A major result of the War on Drugs was a reduction of the voting population, particularly among the young black men. This is because young black men attract a disproportionate amount of attention from law enforcement officials and because convicted felons are barred from voting in many states.

Finally, there are circumstances that can change the entire structure of a political system. This is particularly evident when a revolution occurs, but can also be a product of legislation. A country can move from being an absolute monarchy to being a democracy or a totalitarian dictatorship or election rules can change (as when the United States moved to direct election of senators after the 17th Amendment was ratified in 1913).

The term **economic system** refers to the structure of the economy, including the way goods are produced, the way economic resources are allocated, and who consumes what goods in a society. Changes in the economic system range from the simple (such as small shifts in the per-person income in a society) to the complex (such as shifts in the focus of the economy as a whole). To illustrate, consider the broad implications of the following complex shift: over time, the total quantity of economic resources available to a society may increase or decrease. This is likely to alter the distribution of those resources among different segments of society (e.g., certain people might get more or less of a given resource). When resource distributions change, economic inequality may grow or it may shrink. A concrete example of how this might work involves changes is employment rates. When the percentage of the population that is employed outside of the home grows, there are consequences for society at large. A high employment rate increases economic resources available overall as people earning money (or more money) are likely to spend money (or more money) on goods and services, but it also necessitates that people rearrange their lives, for instance by changing child care arrangements when increased numbers of families have two parents who are both working. On the other hand, if unemployment rates rise dramatically, there are also consequences, both for the individuals who are unemployed and for society at large. An unemployed person is likely to spend less on goods and services (thus affecting the economy as a whole), and society may be forced to change in ways that enable the creation of new social roles for those who are no longer part of the workforce.

The economic sectors in which production is concentrated can be transformed. Economies may concentrate on producing agricultural goods through farming, mineral resources through mining, products through manufacturing, or services with a service-sector economy. These different types of production systems impose very different physical and educational requirements on the population. Now consider how these production systems have changed and evolved over time, what prompted the changes, and how these systemic changes promoted social change. On an even broader level, consider how the basic structure of an entire economy can change; human history has seen many

Per Person Income in the United States, 1929–2009, in Constant 2005 Dollars

Source: Data from the United States Census Bureau and the United States Bureau of Economic Analysis.

© Infobase Learning

such changes as societies have moved from feudal to capitalist or socialist economic structures.

Consider Figure 5, which presents a graph of income per person in the United States. At the lowest point, in 1933, the country was in the depths of the Great Depression, and the entire economic production of the United States generated just $5,705 per person, measured in 2005 dollars. At its highest point, in 2007, the average per capita income was $43,901. Imagine the difference in the standard of living represented by these two figures. For one thing, the homeownership rate in the United States in 1930 was just under 50 percent; in 2007, the rate was 68 percent. For another example, consider how per person income shown in this graph might have affected the amount and quality of food per person or per family.

Of course, the amount of money available in the economy—and the quantity of goods and services that money can purchase—is not the whole story. Economic inequality matters as well. Scholars who study economic inequality use a measure called the **Gini coefficient**. The Gini coefficient measures the proportion of total income earned by those at different points in the income distribution scale. If everyone in a society earned exactly the same income, the

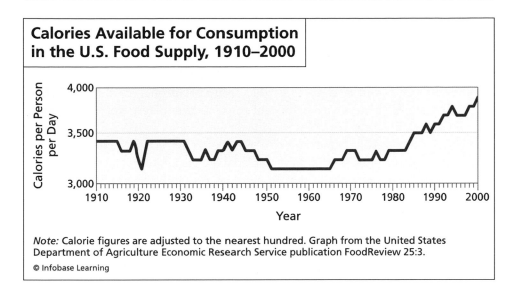

Calories Available for Consumption in the U.S. Food Supply, 1910–2000

Note: Calorie figures are adjusted to the nearest hundred. Graph from the United States Department of Agriculture Economic Research Service publication FoodReview 25:3.

© Infobase Learning

Gini coefficient would be 0. If one person earned all the income and no one else earned anything, the Gini coefficient would be 1 (these, of course, are illustrative examples that are not actually possible in real life circumstances). The Gini coefficient requires strong economic data and, for this reason, is generally used

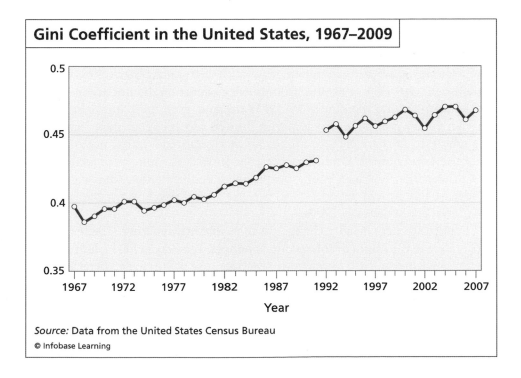

Gini Coefficient in the United States, 1967–2009

Source: Data from the United States Census Bureau

© Infobase Learning

for recent times when technology has made data gathering more sophisticated and comprehensive. It is not readily applicable to earlier time periods.

Consider all of the economic data presented here. We can see that the United States in the early years of the 21st century has many more economic resources than it did in the 1930s—but we can also see that economic inequality has grown. These sorts of economic changes have significant consequences in terms of social change. Our increased economic resources provide us with higher individual standards of living—we can afford, as demonstrated above, better living conditions, more food, and other consumer goods. They have also enabled the United States to invest substantially in the invention and development of new technologies, ranging from new household appliances to advances in prescription drugs, many of which have improved our quality of life. But because of growing economic inequality, not everyone has equal access to these goods. How do you think growing economic inequality has changed our country?

When we talk about the **social structure**, we are talking about the patterns of social arrangements in society, including norms governing social behavior, the connections between people, the different social institutions that exist, and the roles people play as part of social life. At the most basic level, changes in the population within a nation or a region are an example of changes in social structure. When populations grow or decline and when people choose to move into cities or migrate across the globe, the networks of connections between people are reshaped and the ways in which people interact with one another can change. The development of new kinds of formal organizations and new types of social institutions also reshapes social life. For example, consider the development of public schooling in the United States. Until the 1800s, almost all schools in the United States charged tuition; indeed, the first public high school was not established until 1821 in Boston. Compulsory education did not become widespread until around the time of World War I and, even then, was restricted to the elementary grades. In a society with limited access to education—and even one where schools are free for all but are not required—young people would enter the world of work at much earlier ages. Indeed, the concept of adolescence as a time period in which young people are able to function somewhat independently but are not yet adults did not exist until psychologist Stanley Hall popularized it in the early 1900s.

Finally, we can consider changes in the **cultural structure**. The term "culture" refers to the way of life of a group of people. This way of life includes a wide variety of elements, such as religious practices, use of language, dietary habits, entertainment choices, values, and many others. Thus, there are many ways for culture to change—any time there is a change in religious beliefs, language use, food consumption, entertainment practices, or any other element of culture, then culture itself has changed. Though culture can change for many reasons, one of the most common of these is when one culture comes into contact with another and is thus exposed to new ideas and new ways of doing things. This contact can lead to a variety of conflicts between different cultural groups as well as conflicts within cultural groups around whether new practices should be integrated, accepted, or rejected. Similar conflicts can develop as new issues that were previously not discussed become subjects of public discussion, for example sexual practices. Changes in culture, which are in and of themselves social changes, can also create social changes. For example, during the Protestant Reformation, some Protestants developed new religious beliefs that emphasized an individual's responsibility to read and understand scripture themselves rather than following the Catholic practice of depending on priests as intermediaries between the believer and the spiritual world. This combination of cultural changes ultimately led to a decline in the power and influence of the Catholic Church as an organization, but also encouraged an increase in literacy so people could read scripture for themselves.

WHY AND WHEN SOCIAL CHANGE HAPPENS

Social change is always happening. From the earliest history of human society to the present day, societies continue to develop, reshape themselves, and adopt new political, economic, social, and cultural practices and structures. However, many observers of these phenomena argue that the *speed* of social change has increased in recent years. In ancient times, people might go several lifetimes without experiencing a fundamental transformation of some social practice or the development of a significant new technology. In the past few decades, however, it seems like new technologies are being developed every month and that other types of social change happen almost as quickly. This "speeding up" of social change is a symptom of modernity and of globalization (discussed in Chapter 4), but it should not minimize our understanding that change has always been a part of human societies.

So if social change is always happening and has always happened, what produces it? In fact, there are numerous factors that produce social change, and these factors are the basic topic of this book. These factors can be grouped into five broad categories:

1. Economic factors
2. Cultural factors
3. Environmental phenomena
4. Scientific or technological developments
5. Individuals or groups working for change

As discussed above, economic, cultural, and environmental phenomena can all generate social changes. An economic depression or an expansion of

(*continues on page 16*)

The Impact of Technology on Social Life

Technologies of all kinds—from the simplest to the most complex—have had major impacts on humanity. Consider the following examples of technologies that have enabled considerable social change:

Technology	Emergence	Social Change
The Wheel **Front tire of Nissan Fuga.** *(Wikipedia)*	6,000 years ago in Mesopotamia, the Northern Caucasus, and Central Europe. Early wheels were made of wood.	Enabled early societies to move larger quantities of goods than they could carry themselves. Enabled transportation technologies ranging from the horse-drawn carriage to the automobile. This allowed societies to develop long-distance trade and enabled the movement of populations.
The Printing Press **Printing machine.** *(Wikipedia)*	Invented by Johannes Gutenberg around 1440 in what is now Germany. By 1500 printing presses were available throughout Europe.	Dramatically increased the speed at which books and other documents could be produced. This was instrumental in the development of literacy, education, science, Protestant Christianity, the press, and a variety of other social innovations.
Antibiotics **Medical pills.** *(Shutterstock)*	Traditional remedies may have had antibacterial properties, but modern antibiotics were developed by scientists around the world in the 1930s and 1940s.	Antibiotics allowed for the effective treatment of many diseases that had previously been fatal and vastly increased the likelihood that individuals would survive surgery and wounds. Thus, they lowered death rates from epidemics and from war.
The Telegraph **Telegraph.** *(John Schanlaub. Wikipedia)*	Various types of electrical telegraphs were developed in Germany between 1804 and the 1830s.	The telegraph was the first device to allow near-instant communication at distances too far away for visual signals. Thus, they were central in the development of long-distance commercial, social, and political relationships. Some telegraph technology formed the basis for the development of the Internet.

Technology	Emergence	Social Change
The Steam Engine **Model steam engine at the University of Glasglow. This photograph is from Elmer Ellsworth Burns's** *The Story of Great Inventions.* *(Wikipedia)*	Though rudimentary devices with low power output had long been in use, commercial use of steam power began in the early 1700s.	Steam engines were first used to replace waterwheels, allowing factories to be moved away from rivers and facilitating the Industrial Revolution. Later, steam engines were used to power locomotives and ocean liners, increasing the speed and efficacy of long-distance transportation.
The Gun **Colt Single Action Army.** *(Wikipedia)*	Firearms were first used in 12th-century China, where gunpowder was first developed. They reached Europe in the late 1300s. Accuracy and efficacy was limited until the mid-1800s.	Firearms—both those carried by individuals and larger-scale weapons like cannons—vastly increased the scope and scale of war as well as the chance of dying in combat. They also facilitated new and more deadly types of crime.
The Airplane **Lockheed P-80A Shooting Star.** *(Wikipedia)*	The Wright brothers flew 200 feet in 1903. Fighter planes were in use by 1915, during WWI. The first transatlantic flights—and the first commercial flights—took place in 1919.	Airplanes revolutionized transportation. A flight from New York to London today can take as little as 6 hours; even today, boat service takes at least 6 days, and it was slower 100 years ago. Planes also enable speedy mail and freight service as well as permitting military forces to drop bombs from above.

(continued from page 13)
economic productivity can reshape social relationships or lead to the development of new social practices. Changes in cultural life can generate further changes in how people live and what they do. And environmental phenomena, like climate changes and epidemics, can affect the fundamental structure of society, alter our connections to others, and encourage new ways of doing things.

Scientific and technological developments can have similar consequences. Indeed, some research and innovation in science and technology is undertaken specifically with the goal of producing social change. For instance, researchers working on family planning and birth control technology often have the goal of enabling families to have fewer children, a significant change in population dynamics that tends to result in further changes in economies, social practices, and gender relations. But there are many other scientific and technological developments that occur without any explicit intention to change the world. For example, consider the discovery of radioactive elements. Marie Curie, a Polish-French scientist, isolated several important radioactive elements, including radium and polonium, in the course of her scientific research. She made these discoveries without any idea of what their ultimate consequences would be, and indeed was working only to increase our knowledge about physics and chemistry. However, radioactive elements today are used as the basis of many important technologies, including nuclear power, nuclear bombs, and radiation therapy for cancer—all technologies that have had significant impacts on our world.

Social change can also be produced intentionally, when individuals or groups actively seek to change the world. This occurs when people find that there is something about the world that they are dissatisfied with: a cultural practice, political issue, economic structure, or whatever else it might be. They then organize and work with other people to raise awareness about this issue, change people's behavior, and pressure those with the power and influence to enact social change to do so. There are thousands of examples of people coming together to change the world (or their local communities—not all social change has to be worldwide!), some of which will be discussed later in this book. Consider just a few:

- Mahatma Gandhi, who was a major leader in India's struggle for independence from Great Britain, galvanized mass participation in what became a strong resistance movement. Gandhi led a 241-mile march to the ocean to gather sea salt after the British imposed a salt tax. Six thousand people were imprisoned for participating in the march, but the British government reacted by agreeing to negotiate with Gandhi—one of the first steps towards independence.

- The Gay and Lesbian movement in the United States, over the course of just a few decades, was able to change public attitudes about homosexuality—as well as the legal and social treatment of LGBT (lesbian, gay, bisexual, transgender) people—significantly. In the 1950s, same-sex sexual activity was criminal in every state in the United States. Until 1973, homosexuality was considered a mental illness by the profession of psychiatry. Although LGBT people are still discriminated against today, homosexuality is no longer considered a crime or a mental illness. A number of states provide coverage to LGBT in their antidiscrimination laws, and several grant the right to same-sex marriage.
- During the 1968–1969 academic year, students at San Francisco State College (now San Francisco State University) staged a strike to protest treatment of students and instructional staff who were people of color. They demanded courses in ethnic studies and more access to enrollment for nonwhite students, as well as many other things. Students stayed on strike for weeks and the police were called in—but in the end, a School of Ethnic Studies was established on campus.
- In the mid-1800s, factory workers in the United States began to organize into labor unions to demand increases in pay and improvements in working conditions. Some of the earliest trade unionists in the United States were young women working in garment factories, where they earned as little as $1.25 ($23.40 in 2009 dollars) for a week of 17 hour days—with the requirement that they pay for their own needles and thread! With no laws to protect them, workers were fired for organizing—and sometimes were even killed. Yet by the early 1900s they were able to secure considerable improvements in working conditions and pay, including limits on working hours, days off, and compensation for work-related injuries.

Though of course not all efforts to create social change have an impact, these examples show that people working together can and do create significant social change on many fronts. Throughout this book, we will examine the different ways that social change can happen—and the effects of social change—in much more detail.

SOCIOLOGY AND SOCIAL CHANGE

The study of social change is one of the most foundational elements of the discipline of sociology. According to the American Sociological Association, "**Sociology** is the study of social life, social change, and the social causes and consequences of human behavior." Social change is right there in the definition! Indeed, major social change provided the basic intellectual motivation to the

The Founders of Sociology

Founder	Biographical Facts	Examples of Social Change Research
Emile Durkheim	Born 1858 in Lorraine, France. Established first Department of Sociology in the world at the University of Bordeaux, France. Died in 1917.	• Relationship between religion and economic development (*The Elementary Forms of Religious Life*, 1912) • Relationship between social advancement and the maintenance of social order (*The Division of Labor in Society*, 1893)
Karl Marx	Born in Prussia in 1818. Worked in journalism and became involved in radical politics in Paris. Moved to London in 1849 with his primary coauthor, Friedrich Engels. Died in 1883.	• The development of capitalism (*Wage-Labor and Capital*, 1847; *Capital II*, 1885; *Capital III*, 1894) • The development of communism (*Manifesto of the Communist Party*, 1848) • The development of revolution (*The Eighteenth Brumaire of Louis Bonaparte*, 1852)
Georg Simmel	Born in 1858 in Berlin. Lectured in sociology and other disciplines at the University of Berlin. Died in Strasbourg (then Germany) in 1918.	• The consequences of city life (*The Metropolis and Mental Life*, 1903) • The development of and consequences of the money economy (*The Philosophy of Money*, 1900)
Max Weber	Born in 1864 in central Germany. Taught in universities and worked in government. Died in Munich in 1920.	• The development of Protestantism and Capitalism (*The Protestant Ethic and the Spirit of Capitalism*, 1904–1905) • The development of modern social institutions (*Economy and Society*, 1925)

founders of sociology to do the work that would become the core of the new discipline of sociology. Figures like Karl Marx, Max Weber, and Emile Durkheim were writing during a period in which global connections between societies were growing, worldwide military conflicts were brewing, and new technological developments were occurring at unprecedented speeds. Thus, the intellectual project that has become sociology was their attempt to understand the social changes going on around them as they witnessed the Industrial Revolution, the development of capitalism, and the build-up to World War I. Basically, when we study social change we are seeking to understand how the world got to be the way it is today, what processes occurred to get us here, and what we might be able to determine about the possibilities for the future.

Further Reading

American Sociological Association Website. http://www.asanet.org, 2010.

Anleu, Sharyn L. Roach. *Law and Social Change*, 2nd ed. London: Sage Publications, 2010.

Berger, Peter L. *Invitation to Sociology: A Humanistic Perspective*. New York: Anchor, 1963.

Caillods, Françoise, *et al.,* eds. *World Social Science Report 2010*. Paris: UNESCO Publishing, 2010.

Fleisher, Doris Zames, and Frieda Zames. *The Disability Rights Movement: From Charity to Confrontation*. Philadelphia, Pa.: Temple University Press, 2000.

Hall, Stanley Granville. *Adolescence*. New York: D. Appleton and Company, 1904.

Mills, C. Wright. *The Sociological Imagination*. New York: Oxford University Press, 1959.

Noble, Trevor. *Social Theory and Social Change*. New York: St. Martin's Press, 2000.

Sztompka, Piotr. *The Sociology of Social Change*. Oxford, UK: Oxford University Press, 1993.

Weinstein, Jay. *Social Change*, 3rd ed. Lanham, Md.: Rowman and Littlefield, 2010.

CHAPTER 2

POPULATION CHANGE

Consider what the world looked like 500 years ago, around the year 1500. Obviously, the differences between our world and that one are vast: in 1500, Columbus had only recently set sail for the New World, the printing press was only half a century old, and Europe was governed by empires and monarchies. These social changes—globalization, technological change, revolution, and others—will be considered in later chapters. Here, we'll start with an even more basic form of social change: population change. As of August 20, 2010, there were 6,863,631,083 people in the world, according to the U.S. Census Bureau's World Population Clock. That's almost 7 billion people. In contrast, in 1500, scholars estimate that there were between 425 and 540 million people in the world, about one-thirteenth of the number of people alive today. Up until 1500, the human population of Earth had changed slowly; more recently, the human population has expanded exponentially.

This massive growth in the human population has had significant consequences for the state of our world: it has changed where and how we live, it has reshaped our environment, and it has been a key element in many of the other types of social changes discussed later in this book. The study of population change is called **demography**. Demographers study the size, makeup, distribution, and growth or decline of populations as well as the causes and consequences of population change.

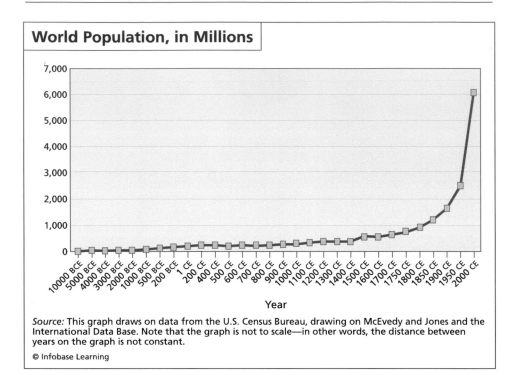

World Population, in Millions

Year

Source: This graph draws on data from the U.S. Census Bureau, drawing on McEvedy and Jones and the International Data Base. Note that the graph is not to scale—in other words, the distance between years on the graph is not constant.

© Infobase Learning

DEMOGRAPHY

The world population grows or declines because of changes in birth (or fertility) rates and death (or mortality) rates. When considering individual populations, like the population of a specific country, migration rates might also be important. There are a number of different ways to measure these factors:

- The **birth rate**, or the number of live births per 1,000 people per year
- The **fertility rate**, or the number of live births per 1,000 women of reproductive age
- The **death rate**, or the number of deaths per 1,000 people per year
- The **infant mortality rate**, or the number of deaths of children age one or under per 1,000 live births per year
- The **life expectancy**, or the number of years an individual can expect to live
- The **immigration rate**, or the number of people who move into a country per 1,000 residents per year
- The **emigration rate**, or the number of people who leave a country per 1,000 residents per year

These various factors are then combined into equations that determine the overall rate of population growth or decline. Population change can be calculated using the formula below:

Population at time 2 =
Population at time 1 + (Births − Deaths) + (Immigration − Emigration)

The picture of population change can be even more complicated than these terms and equations make it seem. The fertility rate, for instance, measures how many children each woman will have. It does not take into consideration how many women there are in a given society, and it does not take into consideration differences in the age at which women have children. Imagine, for instance, that all women have two children in their lifetime—a standard fertility rate. Then consider the differences between the four hypothetical countries described below, all of which start out with a population of 100 people who are all aged 15. For the sake of simplicity, assume that the average woman lives to be 75 in all four countries and that none of the countries experiences any immigration or emigration.

- Country 1 is 50 percent female, and the average woman is 25 when she has her first child. After 100 years, the total population of Country 1 will be 300 people.
- Country 2 is 65 percent female, and the average woman is 25 when she has her first child. After 100 years, the total population of Country 2 will be 390 people.
- Country 3 is 50 percent female, and the average woman is 15 when she has her first child. After 100 years, the total population of Country 3 will be 500 people.
- Country 4 is 50 percent female, and the average woman is 35 when she has her first child. After 100 years, the total population of Country 4 will be 200 people.

So what do these hypothetical scenarios tell us? Well, most importantly that the number of children each woman has—and the number of women in the population—are not the only thing that matters in determining the rate of population growth. The age at which women start bearing children also matters. If women delay childbearing, the entire population will grow more slowly, even if each woman continues to have the same number of children.

Besides equations, demographers also use **population pyramids** to look at the shape and distribution of populations in a society. These are graphs that show the proportion of a nation's population in each age group, separated into women and men. Younger people are at the bottom of the graph and older people are at the top. By looking at the shape of a population pyramid, demographers can tell quite a lot about that society. For instance, a population pyramid that is really shaped like a pyramid, with a broad base and a narrow top, represents a population that is growing. A population pyramid in which the bottom is narrower than the middle is one in which the population has begun to contract. Some populations are fairly stable, meaning that there is neither growth nor decline. Consider the differences between the four population pyramids presented on the next page.

RATES OF POPULATION CHANGE

Thomas Malthus was a British scholar and economist who lived between 1766 and 1834. One of his most famous works, *An Essay on the Principle of Population*, concerned population growth. He believed that agricultural production would continue to expand in a linear fashion while the population would expand exponentially, thus making continuing population growth unsustainable. Malthus thus believed that when population growth outstripped the capacity for agricultural production, famines and epidemics would cause a crisis and a population decline—and indeed for the hundred and fifty years after Mathlus wrote, such a crisis seemed likely. Malthus's proposition came to be known as the **Malthusian catastrophe**, and his work in economics has led many people to refer to economics as "the dismal science." But Malthus's predictions have not come true. Instead, the rate of population increase has slowed in most of the world, while agricultural production has increased substantially. Here one must stop to consider why Malthus's doomsday scenario did not come to pass. What changed?

What Malthus did not realize was the possibility of **demographic transitions**—episodes of demographic change that have significant impacts on global society. These episodes involve significant changes in the rate at which a population grows. Demographic transitions typically involve a significant decline in the death rate, which is followed some time after by a significant decline in the birth rate. It is important to remember that the demographic transition does not result in a global population that is declining. Rather, it results in a population that continues to increase, but at a slower rate than before.

The reduction in the death rate tends to occur because of technological developments that improve nutrition, medical care, and hygiene, among other things. Better nutrition comes about through improved methods of agricultural production that increase crop yields, as well as because of income growth that allows families to purchase more food, better food, and more varied food. Improvements in medical care reduce deaths from childbirth; they also provide access to medicines and vaccines that reduce deaths from common but preventable or treatable conditions like minor infections, measles, and malaria.

Population Pyramids, 2010

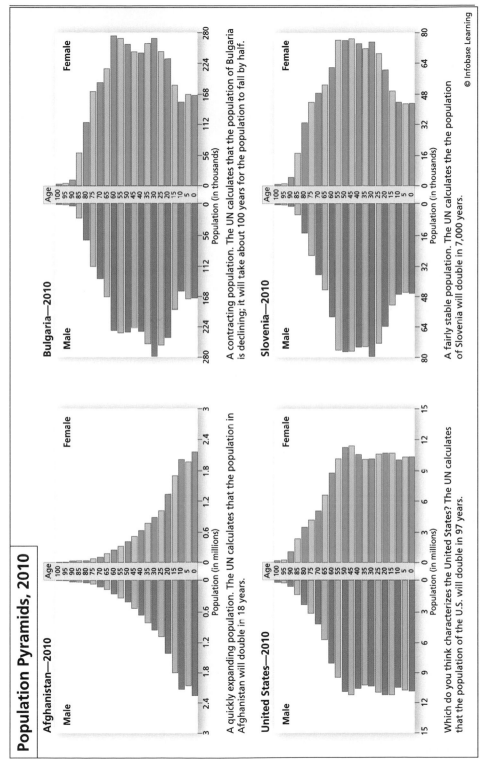

Afghanistan—2010

Male — Female

Population (in millions)

A quickly expanding population. The UN calculates that the population in Afghanistan will double in 18 years.

United States—2010

Male — Female

Population (in millions)

Which do you think characterizes the United States? The UN calculates that the population of the U.S. will double in 97 years.

Bulgaria—2010

Male — Female

Population (in thousands)

A contracting population. The UN calculates that the population of Bulgaria is declining; it will take about 100 years for the population to fall by half.

Slovenia—2010

Male — Female

Population (in thousands)

A fairly stable population. The UN calculates the the population of Slovenia will double in 7,000 years.

Technology sparked by the Industrial Revolution also significantly improved hygiene and safety; sewage systems, pasteurization of milk, and a move away from candles and open fires to electric light and safer forms of heating all increased life expectancy.

In the United States, for instance, the average life expectancy of someone born in 1900 was only 47 (going back to earlier times or to less developed countries would reduce that figure even more); for someone born in 2006 the life expectancy is 77. In 2010, the world average life expectancy was about 67, with some countries (like Japan and Monaco) having life expectancies well over 80.

The demographic transition that began in the developed world at the time of the Industrial Revolution has also been spreading over the last half century or so into the less developed world. Thus, as life-improvement technologies (like pasteurization and malaria control) were introduced to countries around the world, they increased life expectancy on a more extensive scale, thus reducing (or at least stabilizing) the death rate in those countries as well. But this is not a given. In many sub-Saharan African countries, for example, life expectancy remains below 50 (in Angola and Zambia, life expectancy is about 38). When life expectancy increases, changes in the causes of death result as well. Today, about 45 percent of deaths around the world are from cardiovascular diseases or cancers, diseases that tend to be clustered among those who live longer.

All age groups are affected when the death rate declines, but children most significantly. Historically, early childhood mortality was very high, with only a small percentage of children surviving past the age of five. This pattern continues in many contemporary societies with high death rates, and families in these societies respond the way their ancestors did—by having many children to ensure that some will live to adulthood. But as nutrition, medical care, and hygiene reduce infant and early childhood deaths, families find that more and more of their children are surviving. This is one of the first factors relevant to reducing the birth rate.

But there are other incentives for reducing births, including economics and education. In traditional societies, parents relied on children for agricultural labor and to have someone to take care of them in old age; in today's developed countries, where most people work outside the home and have access to retirement savings or social safety nets, children do not serve the same purposes. In addition, greater access to education and to employment opportunities, especially for women, tends to reduce fertility rates. The influence of education on childbearing is evident even in developing countries. For instance, a 35-year study of childbearing in Guatemala found that each additional year of schooling a girl had delayed childbearing by 6 to 10 months and reduced the likelihood that she would have a child before age 18 by 14 to 23 percent. Education also reduces the total number of births women have.

The decline in fertility is partially due to the increased use of fertility control measures like birth control or abortion, but other sorts of family planning that do not rely on fertility control measures are important too. Birth rates decline when women delay marriage or sexual activity or when they simply choose to have fewer children. The decline is greater, of course, where women have access to birth control technology. Today, the countries with the highest fertility rates, which include Afghanistan and many African nations, have 6.5 or more children per woman of childbearing age. Those with the lowest fertility rates are clustered in Eastern Europe and East Asia, with fertility rates under 1.5 children per woman of childbearing age. The United States has a fertility rate of 2.04, close to the **replacement rate** of 2.1. The replacement rate is the number of children each woman in a population would need to give birth to in order for a population to remain exactly the same (when immigration is excluded).

In many developed countries, however, fertility rates have fallen below replacement levels. In countries like Lithuania, Japan, China, and Poland, each woman has fewer than 1.3 children in her lifetime. This means—if one excludes immigration —that such countries will begin to experience population declines. Scholars refer to this as a "second demographic transition," one that has significant consequences for countries that experience it.

Once fertility rates begin to fall, the cultural ideal of family size gets smaller and more adults choose to forgo childbearing entirely, further reinforcing and perpetuating low fertility rates. In countries experiencing population declines, the aging population will have difficulty producing sufficient tax revenues to support retirees, thus leading to significant economic problems. One of the main ways that countries have chosen to respond to this shrinking taxpayer base is by encouraging immigration from countries that are still growing. Such immigration supplies young workers who contribute to tax revenues and support retirees, but immigration is often an unpopular solution to fertility declines. One reason for this is that immigrants evoke the fear of **cultural loss** in a society that is already experiencing some side-effects of decline. In a declining population, for example, people already fear the loss or dilution of their national or ethnic culture; high immigration rates fuel such fears.

The only other solution to the problems created by population decline is to encourage increased rates of childbearing. But this solution has its own limitations. For one thing, a policy of encouraging childbearing can be expensive. Consider, for example, the economics of extended parental leave or subsidized child care. In some European countries with low birth rates, governments have even begun paying families cash subsidies for having second or third children. However, such incentives don't necessarily work. Most families choose the number of children they wish to have and are unlikely to have an additional child because of the promise of a few thousand extra dollars. And for people who delay childbearing because of the many years it takes to complete schooling, develop a career, and afford stable housing, it may be too late to have children in any case. Increasing fertility rates in the developed world also has a major environmental cost. In countries like the United States, Australia, and Canada, carbon emissions per person are over 17 tons annually. In contrast, carbon emissions per person in the higher-fertility countries of Africa are under 0.1 tons annually.

A main determinant of the demographic transition in the less developed world is the **Green Revolution**, a phenomenon that provides one explanation of why Malthus's predictions of crisis and population decline turned out to be wrong. The Green Revolution refers to a series of rapid changes in agricultural production developed in the mid-1900s, which led to dramatic increases in the production of grains like corn, wheat, and rice that serve as staple foods both for humans and for the nonhuman animals that humans use as food. These developments included selective breeding for high-yield crops, the development of industrial harvesting and planting techniques, the wide-spread use of agricultural chemicals as fertilizers and pesticides, and **monocropping** (the planting of single crop over a large area of land). Yields of some crops increased tenfold and prices for food products dropped dramatically. Although the Green Revolution was particularly important in the less developed world, it was part of significant changes in developed countries as well—agricultural production in the United States more than doubled in the past half century, despite far fewer people working in agriculture.

One thing the Green Revolution has not solved is the world's continuing problem with famine. Despite the new heights that agricultural production has reached, many people in the world suffer from malnutrition and starvation. Over 850 million people in the world are chronically hungry, and about 6 million children starve to death every year. Why does this happen? It happens because surplus food, the outcome of the Green Revolution's production of staple crops, does not get to the people who need it. Grain surpluses are produced primarily in developed countries. Less developed countries are often unable to afford the cost of importing food, while developed countries are unwilling to provide food aid. Though the high prices of food have reduced surplus grain storage, as recently as 2001 the U.S. government was storing 777 million bushels of surplus grain acquired through programs designed to subsidize agricultural production. More importantly, much of agricultural production is used for purposes other than feeding people. One quarter of the U.S. corn crop is currently being used to produce ethanol, a car fuel that can replace gas, and the demand for crops to be used in this way has caused food prices to rise substantially. In addition, almost 40 percent of world grain production is used to feed livestock, a much less efficient form of nutrition. In the United States, for instance, livestock production consumes more than 50 percent of the grain harvested and 70 percent of agricultural land. Producing one pound of beef takes about 2,500 gallons of water and 16 pounds of grain and releases 14.8 pounds of carbon dioxide into the atmosphere. In contrast, one pound of soybeans requires 240 gallons of water and releases 0.26 pounds of carbon dioxide into the atmosphere.

ENVIRONMENTAL CHANGE

The discussion above highlights only one way that population growth and the related increase in agricultural production has impacted our environment. Agriculture has many other effects on the environment as well, as does population growth more broadly. Modern agriculture requires large areas of land. These areas of land tend to be created by cutting down trees, and given the desirability of land in areas with warm climates and sufficient rainfall, a lot of **deforestation** occurs, particularly in rainforests. In fact, about half of the forests that covered the Earth in 1946 have now been cut down. Deforestation has a number of negative environmental consequences. Cutting down trees increases the release of carbon dioxide into the air, increasing rates of global warming. Without trees to hold the soil in place, nutrient-rich topsoil erodes, decreasing the productivity of the land. As forests are removed, plant and animal species lose their habitats and thus become endangered or extinct.

As noted above, agricultural production also requires a lot of water. Before the development of modern irrigation technology, it was difficult to grow many crops in dry climates. Today, however, water can be transported from distant areas and used to grow crops in climates without sufficient rainfall. Alongside agricultural uses, more people live in dry climates today, and this contributes to the depletion of fresh water available for human and wildlife use. For instance, Las Vegas averages less than half an inch of rainfall per month and relies heavily on Lake Mead for its water. Researchers estimate that Lake Mead might run dry by 2021 as residents continue to use water to keep golf courses green, fill swimming pools, and keep casino fountains flowing. The Colorado River also supplies water to many communities in the southwestern United States; the river begins in the Rocky Mountains and used to flow all the way into the Gulf of California, but because of irrigation and dams, today it does not consistently reach the ocean. In many dry climates, areas that were previously grassland have been turned into deserts because of the overuse of water, a phenomenon called **desertification**. The overconsumption of water and the resulting scarcity of water in many areas of the world has led to increased conflicts, including military conflicts, and many scholars predict that the wars of the next century will be fought over water. In 2009 alone, for example, significant water conflicts involving violence or the threat of violence erupted in China, Pakistan, India, Ethiopia, and Korea.

Aside from its impact on land and water resources, agricultural production is also a major source of pollution. The Green Revolution introduced large quantities and varieties of chemicals, including fertilizers, pesticides, herbicides, and antibiotics, into agriculture. These chemicals leach into the soil, run off into the water supply, are carried away in the air, and become incorporated into plant and animal tissues. Because of this, most life forms on Earth today are exposed to many chemicals, exposure that can cause the extinction of plant and animal species and cause illness in people who work in or live near the fields or who consume agricultural products. In addition, the use of pesticides and antibiotics has resulted in the evolution of pests and bacteria that are resistant to control efforts and agents, causing major risks to crops and to human health. Of course, agriculture is only one source of pollution. Factories make and use many chemicals as well. When safety procedures are not followed, these chemicals are released into the air and water, further polluting our environment. Individuals are responsible for pollution, too: our cars release pollution into the air, we use chemicals on our lawns and to clean our homes, and we create pollution as we use heat and electricity. Thus, as the population increases, environmental damage is likely to increase as well.

More recent innovations in agricultural production have included genetically modified plant and animal species. **Genetically modified organisms**, or **GMOs**, are plants and animals that have had their genetic makeup altered, often by the insertion of genetic material from another species. GMOs are created to increase yield or pest resistance, to make products sturdier or easier to transport, to add vitamins or minerals to plants, or to increase the profit of agricultural seed companies by forcing farmers to buy seed from particular suppliers. Although advocates of GMOs argue that they will bring about a second Green Revolution, enabling agricultural production to grow more quickly and to continue to supply the world's needs, GMOs bring with them their own risks. Genetic modifications have made some plants sterile, have reduced the number of plant species grown, and have thus created new risks of plant extinction—issues that could begin to have a major impact on the environment as the use of GMO technologies becomes more widespread. Cross-pollination of GMOs with wild crops or non-GMO crops grown by other farmers can lead to the uncontrolled spread of GMO crops into the wild, and we don't know what the consequences of such a spread might be. Researchers also don't know whether GMO crops will have negative effects on human health. Finally, because of the research and development that goes into genetic modification, companies are able to take out patents on GMOs, patents that GMO companies can use to ensure that they make profits by controlling the use of the species they developed. If GMOs do end up having a negative impact on other plants, the results could include a decline in the available food supply and thus a risk of widespread hunger or even starvation.

Organic agriculture, or agriculture that does not involve the use of chemical pesticides, herbicides, some chemical fertilizers, antibiotics, hormones, and genetic modifications, is one alternative to GMOs and a response to the problems discussed above. Indeed, organic agriculture has become more popular as people have become more aware of the impacts of agricultural production on

Reshaping Our World

These images illustrate the impact people have on our natural environment through resource extraction and waste disposal. They show how we are capable not only of creating social change, but also of reshaping the very world in which we live—and not always to good ends.

(clockwise, from top left): Deforestation in Brazil. *(Wikipedia)*; Desertification in the Canary Islands. *(Wikipedia)*; Smog pollution over Mexico City. *(Fidel Gonzalez. Wikipedia)*; Deepwater Horizon Oil Spill in the Gulf of Mexico. *(Wikipedia)*; Landfill in Australia. *(Wikipedia)*; Surface coal mining in Hungary. *(Robert Illes. Wikipedia)*

human health and on the environment. Between 1995 and 2008, the number of acres of agricultural land used for organic production in the United States quadrupled, though certified organic land still accounts for less than one percent of all agricultural land in the United States. Organic trade groups estimate that about 10 percent of all fruits and vegetables purchased in the United States are now grown organically, though consumers remain less likely to purchase organic meat, dairy, and grains. However, even if it expanded considerably, organic production would not solve all of the environmental problems created by agricultural production. Organic livestock production still involves considerable use of water and land. And most agricultural production, whether or not it is organic, takes place far from the sites in which the products will ultimately be used. On average, food products travel 1,500 to 2,500 miles from the farm to the kitchen, and that distance has increased about 25 percent since 1980. For example, a lot of the fresh produce consumed in the northeastern United States in the winter is produced in California or in South American countries like Chile, a distance of 3,000 to 5,000 miles. Every mile that products travel increases their carbon dioxide emissions. Consumers interested in reducing the distance that their food has traveled have created a movement toward local food, buying directly from farmers or at local farmers' markets.

Modern humans also create large quantities of waste. Our waste includes manure from agricultural production, human sewage, leftover materials from industrial production, and trash thrown out by individual households. Some of this waste results in pollution, whether because of chemicals and biological material that run off into rivers or because of toxic products like batteries and gasoline that are disposed of unsafely. Most of it finds its way into landfills or is burned in incinerators. And we produce quite a lot of trash: the average American throws out 4.5 pounds of trash every day, for a total of over 409 million tons of trash discarded a year in the United States in cities alone. According to the United States Department of Energy, 55 percent of trash in the United States is put into landfills, 14 percent is burned, and 31 percent is recycled. Despite the percentage of trash that is recycled today, 22 percent of trash deposited in landfills or burned in the United States in 2007 was paper, 18 percent was food waste, 17 percent was plastic, 16 percent was glass or metal, and 7 percent was yard waste, all products that can be recycled or composted. (Ironically, less than 20 percent of trash comprises products for which recycling is impossible.) All of that trash increases air and water pollution and takes up lots of space in landfills. As these landfills keep growing, some more populated areas have simply run out of room for their own trash. For instance, the Fresh Kills Landfill in New York City is 4.6 square miles in area (some believe it to be the largest human-made structure on Earth). Fresh Kills closed in 2001; today almost of all of New York City's trash is transported out of state, sometimes as far away as South Carolina.

Overconsumption of products is one of the main reasons why we create so much trash. We buy more than we need and throw out the rest. But people today overconsume in other ways too. Overconsumption is responsible for many species becoming endangered or extinct as people hunt and harvest them for food, fashion, or fun, or destroy their habitats. Scientists estimate that as many as 140,000 species of plants and animals may be going extinct each year, and that within 50 years, half of all species on Earth may be extinct. This is not just a theoretical problem—animal extinctions can have a considerable impact on human life. For instance, without major changes in policy and practice, many wild fish species may become extinct in the near future, threatening food supplies and food cultures in many areas of the world.

Other natural resources have become subject to overconsumption as well. These include power sources like oil as well as metals and minerals. Over the

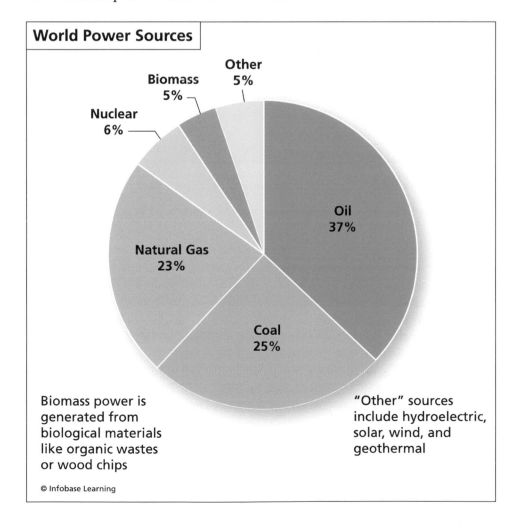

World Power Sources

Other 5%

Biomass 5%

Nuclear 6%

Oil 37%

Natural Gas 23%

Coal 25%

Biomass power is generated from biological materials like organic wastes or wood chips

"Other" sources include hydroelectric, solar, wind, and geothermal

© Infobase Learning

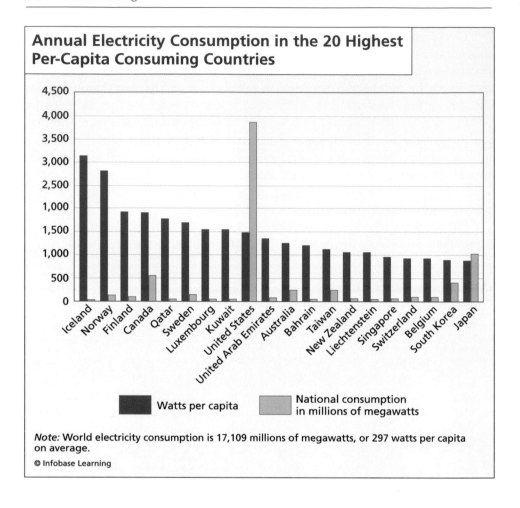

Annual Electricity Consumption in the 20 Highest Per-Capita Consuming Countries

Note: World electricity consumption is 17,109 millions of megawatts, or 297 watts per capita on average.

© Infobase Learning

next 50 years, the world is at risk of running out of metals like silver, tin, gold, and lead, as well as of a number of more rare minerals that are important to the production of medicines and electronics. With currently available technologies, the supply of uranium (necessary for nuclear power) is expected to last 100 to 200 years. And many scholars believe we have already reached **peak oil,** the point at which the rate of oil extraction begins to decline. Easily accessible oil reserves are running out, as evidenced by projects like the deep-water drilling that led to the BP oil leak in the Gulf of Mexico. Oil and natural gas reserves might run out in as little as 40 to 60 years. While there is enough coal to last for a century and a half, mining and burning coal causes significant environmental damage and coal cannot be used for automobile fuel or to make plastics. Today in the United States, 50 percent of our electric power comes from coal, 20 percent from nuclear plants, and 20 percent from natural gas. Renewable energy sources like solar and wind power could reduce these percentages, but renewable energy remains expensive to produce; wind power is also unpopular among some people because of the way the windmills reshape the landscape.

Many of the environmental impacts discussed above relate in some way to the issue of **global climate change**. Although popularly called global warming, this phenomenon is more accurately described by the term "global climate change" because warming is only part of the story. In fact, some parts of the globe are getting colder, like parts of Antarctica and the Pacific Ocean. Climate change is not entirely new. Over the history of the Earth, our planet has experienced many fluctuations in average temperature. During the Ice Age, for example, the whole planet got colder and much of the northern part of what is now the United States was covered in glaciers. Right now, however, our planet is experiencing a change in which the overall average temperature of Earth is rising. What makes this period different from other periods of temperature change is that human activity has been responsible for at least some of the change. By releasing carbon dioxide and other greenhouse gasses into the atmosphere, we have increased the degree to which heat stays at the surface of the Earth instead of radiating into space.

The Intergovernmental Panel on Climate Change predicts that the average temperature of the Earth will increase by 2.5 to 10.5 degrees Fahrenheit by 2100. This temperature change, even though it seems rather small, will have catastrophic effects for many people around the world. As temperatures rise, ice in the Arctic and Antarctic regions melts, causing sea levels to rise. Even a small increase in sea levels could flood island nations like the Maldives and coastal cities like Venice. Once some polar ice melts, the reflectivity of the Earth's surface will decline and even more heat will be retained, accelerating further climate change. While temperature increases and higher levels of carbon dioxide in the atmosphere may promote plant growth, changes in temperature may make regions uninhabitable to species that have lived there for a long time. Some scientists, for instance, believe that a small increase in temperature might kill out oak trees in the Midwestern United States as well as some kinds of coral in the oceans. Temperature increases that make certain regions more hospitable to certain species can also be bad for humans—climate change researchers predict that as temperatures rise, malaria-carrying mosquitoes will reach new areas of the globe. Global climate change will make some regions of Earth more subject to hazardous weather like hurricanes and tornados; other areas will experience significant declines in rainfall that intensify desertification. These changes could threaten human life in many parts of the world. While most scientists think climate change is now irreversible, the speed and extent of climate change may be slowed down and contained if people made major changes in their lifestyles. Such steps could include using less power and burning less greenhouse gases.

The effects of global climate change, along with resource overconsumption, have led some researchers to argue that we are on the brink of a new Malthusian catastrophe. They argue that despite the unprecedented developments in technology and improvements in agricultural production over the past half-century, water conflicts and climate change will begin to reduce agricultural yields in the near future. Coupled with the risk of death from natural disasters and epidemics, both of which might be increased by global climate change, these new Malthusians argue that our planet is reaching its **carrying capacity** (the total number of people that the environment can sustain) and that human populations will decline in the near future. Current estimates predict that we are not likely to face a severe global food shortage in the next two decades, but developing mathematical models that can account for population change, climate change, and agricultural production is a complex task and there is a possibility that these predictions underestimate the potential problem.

URBANIZATION

As the human population has grown, residential patterns have changed as well. As recently as 1800, only 3 percent of people in the world lived in cities; by 1950, 30 percent did. Today, slightly over 50 percent of the world population lives in cities, and the United Nations estimates that that number will rise to 70 percent by 2050. There are many things that differentiate urban life from rural life. The process of moving from rural to urban areas involved people transitioning into wage labor instead of working on the farm. City dwellers then became consumers rather than producers of food and lived in smaller nuclear family groups instead of living with extended family and retaining longstanding community ties.

Though there is no one clear definition of what a **city** is, scholars generally agree that a city is a permanent, relatively large, and densely settled area; typically, city residents are more diverse economically, ethnically, and socially than residents of smaller settlement units. The earliest cities developed in areas we today know as Iraq, India, China, and Pakistan about 7,000 to 9,000 years ago. Even the largest of early cities typically had fewer than 40,000 residents; today, the U.S. Census Bureau requires that a settled area have a minimum of 50,000 people before it can be called a city —and at least some of these people must live at a population density of 1,000 people per square mile or greater. Though there were some very large cities in the past—Rome, for instance, had over a million people by 1 BCE—most cities remained small well into the modern era. In 1950, New York was the only urban area in the world with a population of over 10 million; today, at least 25 cities match this number.

The chart below features the population of the world's 26 largest cities today (as of January 2010)—all of them with a population of over 10 million. The list is rank-ordered from 1 through 26. The chart shows the numerical rank order by population for most of these cities in 1900. Consider where the largest cities in the world are today, where they were in 1900, and where the greatest change has occurred. What do these data tell you about global social change? Note, as well, that five of the cities listed in the column for January 2010 were not rank-ordered in the column for 1900. What factors might be involved here?

Rank, 2010	City	Country	Population, 2010	Population, 1900	Rank, 1900
1	Tokyo	Japan	34,000,000	1,440,121	8
2	Guangzhou	China	24,200,000	1,600,000	7
3	Seoul	Korea	24,200,000	201,000	119
4	Mexico City	Mexico	23,400,000	402,000	47
5	Delhi	India	23,200,000	208,385	109
6	Mumbai	India	22,800,000	770,843	16
7	New York	United States	22,200,000	3,437,202	2
8	São Paulo	Brazil	20,900,000	–	–
9	Manila	Philippines	19,600,000	244,732	91
10	Shanghai	China	18,400,000	380,000	52
11	Los Angeles	United States	17,900,000	102,479	–
12	Osaka	Japan	16,800,000	821,235	15
13	Calcutta	India	16,300,000	949,900	12
14	Karachi	Pakistan	16,200,000	115,047	207
15	Jakarta	Indonesia	15,400,000	116,000	–
16	Cairo	Egypt	15,200,000	570,062	24
17	Beijing	China	13,600,000	1,000,000	13
18	Dhaka	Bangladesh	13,600,000	90,000	–
19	Moscow	Russia	13,600,000	1,039,000	14
20	Buenos Aires	Argentina	13,300,000	663,854	20
21	Istanbul	Turkey	12,800,000	1,125,000	11
22	Tehran	Iran	12,800,000	250,000	88
23	Rio De Janeiro	Brazil	12,600,000	522,651	29
24	London	Great Britain	12,400,000	4,586,063	1
25	Lagos	Nigeria	11,800,000	–	–
26	Paris	France	10,400,000	2,536,834	3

*Note that of the 26 largest cities in the world in 1900, fourteen no longer appear in the top 25 in 2010 (Berlin, Germany; Chicago, Ill.; Vienna, Austria; Philadelphia, Pa; St. Petersburg, Russia; Glasgow, Scotland; Hamburg, Germany; Liverpool, England; Warsaw, Poland; St. Louis, Mo.; Brussels, Belgium; Boston, Mass.; Naples, Italy; and Manchester, England). Data for 2010 are taken from http://www.citypopulation.de and include the entire metropolitan area of which the city is part; data for 1900 are taken from The World Almanac and Encyclopedia from 1902 and represent the most recent Census data included in that text; they does not include surrounding suburbs. Data for 1900 for Los Angeles are taken from the US Census Bureau; for Jakarta they come from Abeyasekere's Jakarta: A History; for Dakha they come from the International Institute for Environment and Development. Where a dash (–) appears, data are not available.

The process by which the global population has changed from largely rural to largely urban is referred to as **urbanization**. Urbanization really refers to a growth in the proportion of the population and the proportion of the land area in a country, region, or the whole world that is urban (that is, centered in cities)—this can be either through an increase in the extent or size of urban areas or through an increase in the density of urban areas. Since the development of settled human agriculture, there has always been urbanization, but it used to be small and slow. Recently, as you can see from the statistics presented in the chart above, the speed and extent of urbanization has expanded dramatically.

So what has led to the dramatic increase in urbanization over the past century? First of all, demographic change in general. As population growth escalated, populations in many rural areas became too massive for those environments to sustain. This process was further intensified by the environmental damage created by industrial agriculture as well as by the decision of wealthy landowners to transform their land into plantations or estates rather than having small-scale farmers work the land. Manufacturing, service, and knowledge work—cornerstones of the modern economy—are all concentrated in cities, and thus people who wanted or needed to work in these industries had to move to cities to get work. Once a significant number of people begin to move to cities for economic reasons, cities become even more attractive to others. The large populations that concentrate in cities create further economic opportunities for landlords, restaurant owners, entertainers, and others. Migrants are also attracted to cities by the diversity of inhabitants and by the availability of activities and resources (such as hospitals and schools) created as a response to population density. Finally, as people settle in cities and begin to build families, populations grow even more. Each of these components serves as a reminder that population growth stems from natural increase from births as well as increases due to migration.

All cities have one thing in common, and that is that they are larger and more densely populated than other areas. But within the category "city," there is considerable variation. Places we call cities can range in size from the 34 million people that make Tokyo home, to cities with fewer than 200,000 people. Although the U.S. Census Bureau stipulates that at least some part of all metropolitan areas (their term for cities) must have a population density of 1,000 people per square mile, this is only a lower boundary on population density. Manila, in the Philippines, is the densest city in the world, with over 111,000 people per square mile; the densest city in the United States is Union City, New Jersey, with about 53,000 people per square mile. The geographical space cities take up varies, too: the largest city in the world by area is Hulunbuir, Mongolia, where 2.7 million people share 101,913 square miles of land; in the United States, the largest city in area is Anchorage, Alaska, where 260,283 people share 1,697 square miles of land. In contrast, the densely populated Union City, New

Jersey, occupies just 1.25 square miles. But cities vary in many ways beyond size and population density.

Especially important are the differences between rich cities, especially rich cities in the developed world, and poor cities, especially those in less developed countries. Though both rich and poor cities can be very densely populated, poor cities are much more overcrowded, as investment in housing does not keep up with population increases. In contrast, rich cities are able to develop housing that meets the needs of the population, without sacrificing air and space. As a consequence of this, poor cities offer fewer sanitation services like sewers, trash collection, street cleaning, and treated city water that can keep even crowded spaces healthy and hygienic. Poor cities are also less able to offer residents access to health care, social services, and other resources, whereas rich cities can offer these things along with a diversity of cultural and entertainment opportunities. Finally, despite the fact that people migrate to poor cities because they see economic opportunities are limited or do not exist in the rural areas they came from, poor cities have more limited economic opportunities than do rich ones. In poor cities, many residents may have to resort to begging or working in marginal sectors of the economy to get by; in rich cities much more stable employment is available—even if it is low-paid work. The majority of the world's urban areas are poor cities, which are already overcrowded and which are continuing to grow, so when we consider the benefits of living in a city in the developed world—access to jobs, entertainment, social services, and a diverse social life— we need to remember that this is not the dominant experience of city residents in the world.

When we view urbanization as a form of social change, we do not look only at demographic changes. Urbanization (and the cities it enlarges) also has considerable environmental and social consequences. Cities increase the pressure of population on the land—they increase use of water, food, space, and other resources, and they also increase the distance that resources like food and water must travel in order to reach people. Pollution from industry, traffic, and human waste are also concentrated in cities and can have negative health effects on humans and other life forms; lives and health are also at risk from accidents like traffic collisions or building collapses. As cities expand and grow, they often encroach upon and destroy wild habitats and ecosystems, with a particular effect on wetlands that may be drained for building or to supply cities with water. Finally, many researchers have raised concerns that cities create distance and separation between people and nature. As more and more generations grow up in cities, we lose knowledge about plant and animal life and may become less inclined to protect it. In addition, spending time in natural and green spaces has positive effects on people's mental states—indeed, researchers have found that hospital patients who can see trees from their windows recover faster than those without such a view. Some cities maintain parks and other green spaces; others, for lack of space or lack of funding, do not. Residents of the latter may have no access to nature at all.

When people are concentrated in dense urban areas, health and crime risks can spread more rapidly. In crowded areas, epidemics spread much more easily, and this is especially true where hygiene and sanitary facilities are poor. However, health care may also be more accessible in cities than in surrounding areas, giving those who do become injured or ill a better chance of survival. Even if crime rates per person are no higher in cities than in surrounding areas, the increased density in cities leads people to feel that more crime is occurring and thus to fear crime in their everyday lives. As an example, consider this comparison: A town with a population of 5,000 people and a city with a population of 500,000 people both have a violent crime rate of 8 crimes per 1,000 population per year. In the small town, that means 40 violent crimes will occur in a year, or about one every 9 days. In the city, 4,000 crimes will occur, or about 11 every single day. Even though residents are equally as safe (or unsafe) in both place, these statistics feel different to people who hear about crimes more often.

Living in cities also changes the way that people interact with one another. Georg Simmel, one of the founding theorists of sociology, wrote about these changed dynamics by describing what he called the **metropolitan man**. The metropolitan man lives in an environment in which work is specialized and each person does a specific task—what we call the **division of labor**. Rational and objective thought are valued, while subjective thought, opinions, and emotions are not valued as guides for how to live. Time and measures of weight or distance are standardized, enabling things like train schedules. So far, these characteristics have much in common with those of modernity and bureaucracy, phenomena you will read about later in this book. But there are further characteristics of the metropolitan man that are unique to city life. For the metropolitan man, Simmel argues, neighbors are all strangers and all relationships are mediated by money. Unlike living in a smaller community, where you spend your whole life knowing the people around you and where the grocer may be your next-door neighbor and the doctor is someone you went to school with, in the city you don't know the people around you at all, and when you need something, you get it only if you can pay. One consequence of the stranger phenomenon is the freedom to be yourself as an individual without facing the risks of negative comments and social sanctions that you might face in a smaller community. Many people do migrate to cities for just that freedom, whether because they wish to choose a different religion, a different lifestyle, or even something as simple as a different way of dressing. Of course, this freedom has social costs as well, in that people are less able to depend on one another for social support and assistance. The final element of Simmel's metropolitan man model is what Simmel calls the **blasé attitude**, in other words a lack of reaction to even the most outrageous things going on around us. Someone exhibiting the blasé attitude would, for example, not notice if a circus clown with a pink poodle walked by, because so much of urban life is already outrageous. This is a marked contrast with life in a smaller and more stable community, where even a conventional-looking person who happens to be a newcomer to town would attract quite a lot of attention.

SUBURBS

In response to some of the environmental and other discomforts of cities, a new form of geographical and residential arrangement developed in the last century: the **suburb**. Suburbs have lower population densities than cities (often mandated by zoning laws) and must be located close enough to cities to allow suburban residents access to jobs and other services within cities. Although people have always lived on the outskirts of cities, the places we would recognize as suburbs really began to develop in the United States after World War II. A combination of rising numbers of young families in need of housing, increased access to personal cars and public transportation, a new interest in zoning laws, and government investment in development through housing loans made via the GI Bill and the Federal Housing Administration led to a boom in suburban construction. The first large-scale suburbs were built in Long Island in New York State, and they rapidly expanded across the country as middle class families moved away from urban areas that they associated with crime and disorder. Today, slightly more than 50 percent of people in the United States live in suburbs, about 20 percent live in rural areas or villages, and the remainder live in cities. Of course, sub-urbanization has not been limited to the United States; Canada, Malaysia, and China are examples of other countries with growing suburban developments. In contrast, the suburbs surrounding many European cities like Paris or Rome are primarily populated by poor people and recent immigrants rather than the middle-class families we associate with suburban living in the United States.

Although the growth of cities was a remarkable change in human social organizations, suburbs represent an even further change in how people live their lives. Consider how urban, village, rural, and suburban life compare in terms of size, density, diversity, economy, inequality, community, and current rates of population change.

Like any way of life, suburban living has its own particular consequences for social and economic life and for the environment. Suburbs feature single-family homes with landscaped yards. Grass lawns, which homeowners even in dry regions seem to prefer, are suited to a rainy climate, so homeowners water their lawns—a practice leading to overconsumption and depletion of water resources in many suburbs. Suburbs also feature low-density populations with relatively large plots of land for each home; shopping tends to be in malls and shopping centers rather than in mixed-use developments where stores share buildings with offices or apartments. This sprawl means that fewer people take up more

	Urban	Village	Rural	Suburban
Size	Large	Small	Any size	Any size
Population Density	Very Dense	Somewhat Dense	Sparse Population	Population Sprawl
Diversity	All forms of diversity are high	High age diversity; other types are low	High age diversity; other types are low	Little diversity of any kind
Economy	Varied—all kinds of economic activities except agriculture	Varied—agriculture, merchants, & artisans	Predominantly agriculture	Little—most people commute to work elsewhere
Inequality	High inequality within area	Some inequality within area	High inequality within area	High inequality comparing areas
Community	Little community; most interactions are with strangers	Tight community; neighbors know one another	Tight community, though across long distances	Little community; few interactions with anyone
Population change	Increasing in less developed countries and major cities; decreasing elsewhere	Decreasing in most cases	Decreasing substantially	Increasing in high-growth areas; stable elsewhere

land than they would in a city, thus leading to widespread habitat loss for many forms of wildlife and increased conflicts between humans and wildlife. Such conflicts might include collisions between cars and deer on the roads, bears who are attracted to human garbage, and small animals who dig up people's gardens. As these animals lose forested and rural areas in which to live, they are forced into suburban developments where they compete with humans for space and resources. Habitat loss also occurs because of the clear cutting of forests, whether for building sites or to get more wood for new homes—a practice that further increases the risk of global climate change.

Suburban sprawl has also reshaped the transportation system. Few suburbs are built with good sidewalks or convenient public transportation, and even where such amenities are available, long distances between homes in residential neighborhoods and the commercial areas where residents shop or the cities where they work means that people turn to private cars for transportation instead. Today, the average worker in the United States spends about 25 minutes commuting to work each way; in New York City, the average worker commutes about 40 minutes each way, and almost 5 percent of commuters commute for more than 90 minutes each way. Ninety percent of all commuters travel by car, and almost all of them drive alone rather than carpooling. As of 2001, only 15 percent of kids who lived within one mile of their schools rode bikes or walked to school. Although similar statistics are not available about how we travel to shop or for entertainment, the patterns are probably similar. These transportation patterns increase pollution and global climate change and also increase our use of resources like gas. In addition, many scholars believe that the increased car use and decreased walking that comes with suburban living has been responsible for growing rates of obesity, along with diabetes, heart disease, and other conditions.

Beyond environmental impacts, suburbs have consequences for our social and economic lives. While suburban residents often face long commutes to their

For a sense of what suburban sprawl looks like, consider this aerial view of Levittown, Pennsylvania. William Jaird Levitt was a real estate developer who built planned communities in New York, Pennsylvania, New Jersey, Puerto Rico, Maryland, Virginia, and Florida. These communities had thousands of identical houses built assembly-line style over many acres. *(Library of Congress)*

jobs in the city, jobs that pay well and require advanced education and training, low-paid service jobs like those in stores, restaurants, house cleaning, and garden work move out of the city and follow the population into the suburbs. But the people left behind in the city often cannot afford to move to the suburbs to follow these jobs, and they do not have access to transportation to the suburbs that would enable them to find work. As a consequence, suburbanization has led to economic depressions in many inner-city areas. Those residents of the suburbs who are themselves poor have trouble accessing medical care, jobs, and other resources, hindered by economic constraints and transportation problems. Because suburban communities lack the social ties of village and rural life, people do not have neighbors to turn to for help in emergencies. Finally, suburbs lack diversity, and thus suburban residents tend to have little interaction with people unlike themselves.

Suburbanization is even implicated in the economic recession that occurred at the end of the 2000s. One of the main factors leading to this recession was the sub-prime mortgage crisis. **Sub-prime mortgages** are home loans given to people who would otherwise not qualify for loans. As long as home values go up, such people will always be able to sell their home for a profit even if they cannot afford to pay their bills. But as home values began to fall, people with sub-prime mortgages were unable to resell their homes or pay their bills, and thus banks foreclosed on their homes and evicted them. Of the top 50 zip codes in foreclosure rates in 2008, all but one was a suburban neighborhood (the remaining one was a rural zip code); many were in areas that had been recently developed into sprawling new suburbs. Some such areas are now largely deserted, as the fall in home prices has made them unattractive to new homebuyers while their prior residents can no longer afford to live there.

RESPONDING TO POPULATION CHANGE

Population growth, urbanization, and suburbanization have had, as we have seen, major consequences for humans and for the environment. Many scholars and activists have proposed ways to respond to the fallout of these phenomena in ways that might limit their continuing impacts on our world. For instance, those concerned with the impact of growing human populations on Earth and the potential for a Malthusian catastrophe encourage **zero population growth**, a practice that would limit the birth rate in a society so that it does not exceed the death rate and thus stop population growth. In most developed countries, zero population growth would require that women give birth to an average of 2.1 children each (discussed above as the replacement rate); because of higher death rates in the developing world, the replacement rate there would be closer to 3 children per woman. As we have seen, fertility rates in many developed countries have already dropped to replacement rates or below, but fertility rates in other parts of the world remain high. China's one-child policy, which encourages people to wait until they are older to have children and permits only one child for most urban couples (most rural couples are permitted to have two), was a way of responding to high fertility in that country and moving towards zero population growth. Many people disapprove of the one-child policy because they see it as inappropriate for the government to dictate personal decision making. Moreover, because of a cultural preference for male children, the one-child policy has been partially responsible for a gender imbalance in China. In most developed countries, there are 107 male births for every 100 female births (sex ratios equalize later in life, as boys are more likely to die in childhood), but in China, there are 119 male births for every 100 female births. Controversy aside, policies like this do have the potential to halt or reverse population growth. Today, demographers predict that China will reach zero population growth by 2030. But fertility rates can be reduced even in the absence of official policies. Increasing women's access to health care, birth control and family planning services, and education would also serve to reduce the number of children that women want to have and the number that they actually do have.

Another response to the problems of population growth has to do with decreasing our use of resources, whether through conservation, reuse and recycling, or new technological developments. Conservation simply means using fewer resources. For instance, if people switch to public transportation or walk instead of driving cars, they will conserve gas. Reuse and recycling allows products to find a new life instead of being discarded in landfills. Today's technology makes it possible to recycle most plastics, and many craftspeople find new uses for old fabrics and household objects. Finally, new technologies allow us to use fewer natural resources. Hybrid and electric cars use much less gas. Energy-efficient light bulbs, like those using LED technology, reduce our use of electricity. And alternative energy sources like wind or solar power are renewable and make us less dependent on nonrenewable fossil fuels.

Regional planning can redesign urban, suburban, and rural communities to lower their negative environmental and social impacts. Better public transportation can reduce pollution and resource use while encouraging more exercise, less stressful commutes, and better access to job opportunities. Residential neighborhoods can be designed to include sidewalks, mixed-use facilities with local shops, and front stoops that encourage socializing. Cities and regions can commit to preserving open space for farms, forests, and parks. Tax policies can even be used to encourage land owners to prevent open space and farmland from being sold and used for further suburban development. And agricultural scientists and policy makers can work to reduce the negative environmental and social impacts of industrial agriculture by encouraging more local farming, a greater diversity of crops, and a reduction in chemical pesticides and herbicides. Later chapters in this book will discuss the dynamics of reform and of social movements—the processes necessary for making changes like these a reality.

Further Reading

Baldassare, Mark. *Trouble in Paradise: The Suburban Transformation in America*. New York: Columbia University Press, 1986.

Bennett, Michael, and David W. Teague, eds. *The Nature of Cities: Ecocriticism and Urban Environments*. Tuscon: The University of Arizona Press, 1999.

Centers for Disease Control. National Vital Statistics System, *National Center for Health Statistics*. http://www.cdc.gov/nchs/nvss.htm (accessed August 22, 2010).

Central Intelligence Agency. *The World Factbook*. https://www.cia.gov/library/publications/the-world-factbook (accessed August 22, 2010).

Goudie, Andrew. *The Human Impact on the Natural Environment*. Malden, Mass.: Blackwell Publishing, 2006.

Greenberg, Paul. "Tuna's End." *The New York Times Magazine*, MM28, June 22, 2010.

Imhoff, Daniel, ed. *Farming with the Wild*. Berkeley, Calif.: University of California Press, 2003.

Malthus, Thomas. *An Essay on the Principle of Population*. London: J. Johnson, 1798. Library of Economics and Liberty. http://www.econlib.org/library/Malthus/malPop.html (accessed August 22, 2010).

Murphy, Elaine, and Dana Carr. "Powerful Partners: Adolescent Girls' Education and Delayed Childbearing." *Population Reference Bureau*. http://www.prb.org/pdf07/powerfulpartners.pdf. (accessed August 22, 2010).

Pollan, Michael. *The Omnivore's Dilemma*. New York: Penguin Group, 2006.

Rowe, Peter G. *Making a Middle Landscape*. Cambridge, Mass.: The MIT Press, 1991.

Simmel, Georg. "The Metropolis and Mental Life." In *The Sociology of Georg Simmel*, edited by Kurt H. Wolff, 409–424. New York: The Free Press, 1950.

Smith, Alisa, and J.B. Mackinnon. *Plenty: Eating Locally on the 100 Mile Diet*. New York: Three Rivers Press, 2007.

Stilgoe, John R. *Borderland: Origins of the American Suburb, 1820–1939*. New Haven, Conn.: Yale University Press, 1988.

U.S. Census Bureau. "International Programs." *U.S. Census Bureau Population Division*. http://www.census.gov/ipc/www/ (accessed August 20, 2010).

Weber, Karl, ed. *Food, Inc*. New York: Public Affairs Books, 2009.

Weeks, John R. *Population: An Introduction to Concepts and Issues*. Belmont, Calif.: Wadsworth Publishing, 2007.

Weinstein, Jay. *Social and Cultural Change: Social Science for a Dynamic World*, 2nd ed. Lanham, Md.: Rowman and Littlefield, 2005.

CHAPTER 3

TECHNOLOGICAL CHANGE

Imagine your life if you had been born a century earlier. There would be no refrigeration, no air conditioning, and no separation of sewage from drinking water. Unless you were very wealthy, you would not live in a house with electric power and you would not have access to an automobile. If you moved to a different country, you might never see your family again or even hear their voices: neither the airplane nor transcontinental telephone wires existed a hundred years ago.

We might think 100 years is a long time—certainly, it's longer than we expect to be alive—but even if you imagine life 20 years ago, things are very different. Twenty years ago there was no Internet, and most people did not have computers or cellular phones. In 1990, if you wanted to be in touch with a friend or relative who lived across the country, you had to mail a letter or spend 16 cents a minute for a long-distance phone call. You would have listened to most of your music on cassette tapes, taken film to a store to have it developed into photographs, and if you got lost, you would have had to stop and ask for directions instead of using a GPS device.

Moore's Law (which is not really a law, but rather an observation about technological advancement made by Thomas Moore in 1965) states that the number of transistors on a computer chip doubles every two years. Transistors and chips are the building blocks of computer processors, and thus Moore's law tells us that every two years, computers can work twice as fast, or alternatively, that a computer with the same power can be half the size. A related point was made by David House, the CEO of Intel in the 1980s, who argued that computer performance would double every 18 months, an observation that seems to have been close to the truth. Moore's law tells us why it is possible for computers to shrink as much as they have. In 1965, when Moore was writing, computers were the size of an entire room and might take all night just to perform a simple task. The IBM System/360 Model 91 computer was used at NASA in the late 1960s. It would have had up to eight megabytes of memory (roughly enough to store two songs today) and run at a speed of about 1 MIPS (million instructions per second). Today's computers can run at 50,000 or more MIPS. Data that did not fit in the computer's internal memory were stored on large spools of magnetic tape, and programs were run by using cards with holes punched in them. Though the IBSM System/360 model 91 kept entire teams of scientists busy by making previously impossible computations, its capabilities look trivial today when compared to devices like DVD players and programmable ovens. While Moore's law addresses speed rather than storage, a similar principle can be illustrated if you consider the difference between the original iPod and newer models. The first iPod, released in 2001, could store 1,000 songs in a device that weighed 6.5 ounces; the newest iPod shuffle can hold almost as many songs in a device that weighs 0.38 ounces.

We know that all of these things are technology related, but what does technology really mean? **Technology** refers to tools and procedures that let humans control or modify the natural world. When social scientists use the word "technology," they are referring both to things we now see as simple, like the wheel or the hammer, and to more modern technologies. Modern technology tends to be defined by four characteristics:

1. It is *complex*—difficult to understand and difficult to create. For instance, think of the cell phone, a technology that is common around the world today. How many of us really understand how the cell phone works, and how many of us could make one ourselves?
2. It involves *dependency*. Technologies depend on other technologies, so that one cannot exist without the others. For instance, think of the Internet. The Internet could not exist without computers, which in turn could not exist without electricity.
3. It involves *variation*. Many different types of items with the same general purpose will be developed. For instance, think of the car. Over 300 different car models are available each year just in the United States alone, but all of them work similarly to get you from point A to point B.
4. Finally, modern technology is *large in scale*. It affects every area of life, and in fact it comes to dominate our existence. Just think about how hard it is for some people you know to go a few days without

The Consequences of Contemporary Technological Change

The pace of technological change in our contemporary world is faster than it has ever been before. Just think of technologies that were not widely available— or had not been invented yet—even in the year 2000: smartphones (cell phones with advanced computing power), Facebook, YouTube, iPods, high definition television (HDTV), Skype, and the full sequence of the human genome, for example. These and the many other technological innovations and inventions that have characterized recent human history have been the subject of a lot of debate and discussion. All of this new technology has made much more information available to us and has thus increased our knowledge about the world and our ability to make further technological advances. For some, this means that technological development is a good thing. But others are not so sure. They point to the fact that technological development can lead to **information overload**, a situation in which people can no longer process new information or make decisions because there is too much information or because they face too many potential choices. Others claim that technologies like iPods and Facebook lead to social alienation as people spend all of their time in front of the computer instead of interacting in real life with others. Think about the last time you hung out with your friends—how much of the time were they staring into their cell phones or computer screens?

checking their cell phones, their email, or their favorite social networking Web sites.

Technological change is a big part of social change. Changes in technology reshape our social lives in many ways—the airplane, the telephone, and the Internet have made it possible for people to stay in touch across continents; the washing machine, clothes dryer, and refrigerator have lessened the amount of housework that people do; and the automobile and electric power have changed the way we work, the way we play, and the impact that we have on the environment. So how and when has technological change occurred?

INDUSTRIALIZATION

Industrialization refers to the process of moving from a society with little technology, low levels of **economic capital**, and an economy governed by farming and small craft production to a society with significant technological development, higher levels of economic capital, and an economy governed by manufacturing and large-scale production. In Europe and North America, industrialization occurred during a period we call the **Industrial Revolution**,

The Timeline of Human Existence

When do you think "human society" began? A commonly used estimate is when the first human-like animals who used tools were alive—about two million years ago. The diagram below starts with the development of Homo Erectus, a key ancestor of modern humans. But even a 10-foot long timeline starting with Homo Erectus does not give us space to mark such important events in human history and technological change as the emergency of Christianity, the invention of the printing press, the development of modern warfare, the European discovery of the New World, the Industrial Revolution, and the American Revolution. On this ten-foot long timeline, the years since the Industrial Revolution would take up about one fiftieth of an inch. Yet these are the precise changes we think of as fundamental to what human society is today!

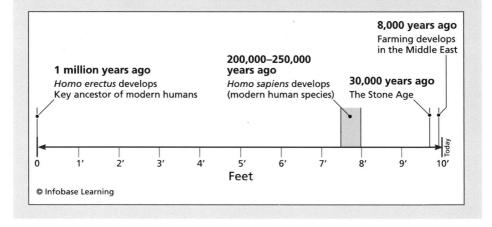

© Infobase Learning

between the 1750s and the early 1900s. Perhaps the most important technological change that was part of the Industrial Revolution was the invention of the steam engine. The steam engine allowed transportation and manufacturing to move away from using humans and animals as power sources, and thus rapidly increased the speed of both. The Industrial Revolution also resulted in the invention of the **assembly line**, in which workers each performed a very small part of the manufacturing process and quickly produced a great number of identical products. Finally, the Industrial Revolution involved massive improvements in agricultural technology that made it possible to feed more people using less farmland, thus freeing up a greater percentage of the population for work in manufacturing industries.

Industrialization has led to many other changes in human society. It is related to the emergence of **capitalism** as a form of economic organization, the development of **bureaucracy**, and even changes in how we fight wars! Let's

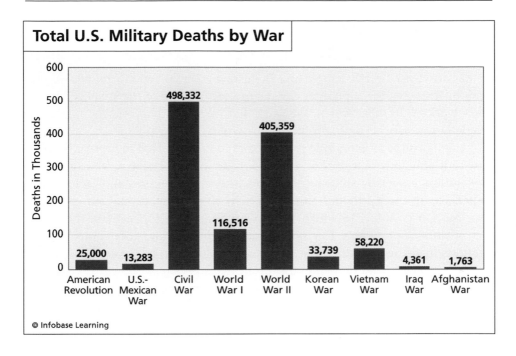

consider this last point. Modern, industrialized wars are more global in scope than previous wars, because we have military technology (like warships and airplanes) that allow soldiers to travel pretty much anywhere in the world. As industrialized war first developed, death rates dramatically increased because of the development of new and accurate weapons (e.g., guns, canons, and bombs); later, death rates decreased due to the development of advanced medical care that allowed soldiers to survive even severe injuries. Modern wars also involve many more civilians than earlier wars did. During the American Revolution, for example, lines of soldiers faced each other on a battlefield and began shooting on command. Today, warfare is often a matter of aerial bombings, which do not discriminate between soldiers and civilians.

This graph shows how the fatality rate of U.S. soldiers increased as war modernized—and then decreased as medical technology made it possible for badly injured soldiers to survive their injuries. Do note that in the Civil War American soldiers were fighting on both sides of the conflict, the main reason the fatality rate is as high as it is.

CAPITALISM

The Industrial Revolution and the technological changes it inspired are closely related to the spread of **capitalism** as an economic system. Karl Marx described capitalism as an economic system in which workers sell their labor power to capitalists (the people who own businesses) in return for cash wages that the workers then use to secure the things they need to survive, like food and shelter. This system is different from earlier economic systems which were generally characterized by individuals working on small farms or their own small businesses and thus directly supporting themselves. Under capitalism, people who own businesses—the capitalists—make money because of the surplus labor of their workers. In other words, the work that workers do beyond the minimum needed to survive becomes profit for the owner.

Capitalism as an economic system emerged and evolved in Europe between the 15th and 18th centuries and played a key role in enabling the Industrial Revolution, especially since technologies like steam engines and factories are expensive. In theory, though not necessarily in practice, capitalism involves a **free market** economy in which the government does not regulate the activities of workers or owners. Decisions about production and about consumption are thus made by individuals or companies rather than by government, prices are set by supply and demand, and property is privately owned. One feature of capitalist economies is economic inequality, because capitalists have more money than their workers (often much more money). Some people argue that this inequality serves to motivate technological change and development by providing economic incentives and rewards for innovation, but it is possible for technology to develop in noncapitalist systems and environments that have alternative motivators and rewards in place.

BUREAUCRACY
Another key social development related to industrialization and technological change is **bureaucracy**. Max Weber, one of the founders of the discipline of sociology, laid out six key characteristics of bureaucracies: division of labor, jobs separate from job holders, stable and hierarchical authority structure, rules and records maintained in writing, education and training for workers, and action governed by rational thought. For illustrative purposes, let's consider how each of these characteristics might apply to a typical American public high school.

Bureaucracies are characterized by a **division of labor** based on specialized skills, roles, and tasks. So in a high school, there is one teacher specializing in English and a different teacher specializing in math. If students misbehave or get in trouble, teachers send them to a counselor or principal, whose specialties include dealing with such problems. Other staff clean the building and serve the lunches.

In a bureaucracy, jobs are separated from job holders. This means that people hold their jobs because of their qualifications, not because of who they are; their jobs tend to have some separation from their private lives; and they are paid for their work. In high school, teachers are hired to work at the school, receive pay for their work, and go home to their families at night. This might seem fairly obvious, but it was not always the way things worked. Before the development of modern bureaucracies, a tax collector could purchase his job from the king and in return get to keep all the taxes he collected. As another example, apprentice blacksmiths would be selected on the basis of personal relationships rather than qualifications.

Bureaucracies have stable and hierarchical authority structures, and there are rules about how things work. Workers who follow the rules and do their jobs well have the possibility for upward mobility. In our high school example, the teachers work for department heads or assistant principals, who then report to principals. These principals in turn answer to superintendents and school boards. Each position is governed by a set of written rules, and workers who are good at their jobs and have the required educational credentials might get promoted to the next level.

Bureaucracies maintain their rules and records in writing. People know what the rules are and follow them. High schools often have a written student code of conduct; teachers will be given a similar employee handbook; and students' grades are regularly recorded on official transcripts.

In order to get a job in a bureaucracy, workers need education and training. Education for bureaucratic jobs is less about acquiring knowledge and culture and more about **credentialing**, or establishing that an individual has the qualifications for the job. So in order to be an English teacher, an individual must demonstrate that she or he has the credentials to be a teacher by completing a college or graduate degree and passing a certification test. This test does cover a lot of areas of knowledge related to working as an English teacher—but it does not require that the potential teacher be knowledgeable about other subject areas, like geography or foreign languages, knowledge that might have been expected of any educated person fifty years ago.

Bureaucracies are based in **rationality** and rational thought (discussed below) rather than in tradition or emotion. Rationality then dictates how things happen in the bureaucracy. So if you fail a required course, (most) high schools will have you repeat that course—even if you cry and beg to be excused!

Bureaucracy as a form of social organization is closely related to capitalism and to industrialization. Bureaucracies, since they pay workers salaries and generally are large organizations, can exist only in economies that are based on money rather than on trade and barter. Indeed, some of the first bureaucracies developed as part of taxation programs in order to enable the efficient and systematic collection of taxes. The large companies that developed around assembly-line production tend to be run as bureaucracies, with individuals responsible for particular parts of the production process and managers selected on the basis of qualifications. Today, we face bureaucracies in almost all areas of life—our education, medical care, workplaces, religious organizations, and even recreational activities are organized according to the principles of bureaucracy.

RATIONALIZATION

George Ritzer, a noted contemporary sociologist, explained the development of bureaucracy and rationalization in his book *The McDonaldization of Society*. **McDonaldization**, according to Ritzer, is a process by which all of society takes on the characteristics of a fast-food restaurant, becoming standardized and increasingly subject to scientific management (often through the use of new technologies). He takes McDonald's as a key example of these processes because it was one of the first large-scale corporations to fully embrace the process he calls McDonaldization and because it is a large, well-known company with a global popular image. Ritzer's McDonaldization thesis includes four components:

- *Efficiency* (the fastest and cheapest method for getting to the desired result);
- *Calculability* (the emphasis on using quantitative analysis in relation to products and services);
- *Predictability* (the emphasis on ensuring that products and services are identical at all times and in all places); and
- *Control* (the regulation of people and processes, particularly through the use of technology).

The assembly line began to systematize and standardize production technology, but the assembly line did not standardize the work done by employees. Fredrick Winslow Taylor, an engineer, developed a system for standardizing work that has come to be known as **Taylorism**, or scientific management. Using this system, companies develop a model for how each job should be performed and train workers to perform the job according to precise guidelines—sometimes going as far as choreographing workers' movements. If you've ever read the book *Cheaper By the Dozen*, you might remember that the Gilbreth household is run according to principles of scientific management. For example, the Gilbreths filmed ordinary household tasks to determine how "wasted motions" could be eliminated to make cooking and cleaning for their twelve children more efficient. Taylorism is essential to McDonaldization, because it enables companies to know that their products will be produced quickly, cheaply, in large numbers, and in an identical form all around the world.

On a broader level, the process of McDonaldization is an example of **rationalization.** Rationalization is the process through which human social actions become defined by logic and efficiency rather than by emotion, tradition, or custom. In many cases, rationalization relies on new technologies to create that efficiency. Although rationalization makes scientific management possible and was part of the massive expansion of scientific research and industrial production that characterized the 20th century, it can also have negative consequences.

McDonald's in Pine Bluff, Arkansas. McDonald's' business practices were the inspiration for George Ritzer's ideas about McDonaldization. *(Wikipedia)*

Rationalization is related to such social developments as standardized testing, the decline of locally owned businesses, and a lack of emotional connection in the contemporary world.

THE KNOWLEDGE ECONOMY
Today we still talk a lot about the Industrial Revolution and its effects on our lives, but in most developed countries (like Germany, the United States, Canada, Australia, and Japan) we have really moved beyond the Industrial Era. In

Changes in the Global Manufacturing Industry

This graph measures the percentage of **Gross Domestic Product** that comes from the manufacturing sector of the economy in four very different countries in different parts of the world. The Gross Domestic Product (GDP) is a measure of the total economic value of all goods and services produced in a society. As the chart shows, Germany and the United States have experienced significant declines in the percentage of their GDPs that come from manufacturing; in Mexico, there has been a small increase; and in China, the manufacturing percent of the GDP has increased significantly.

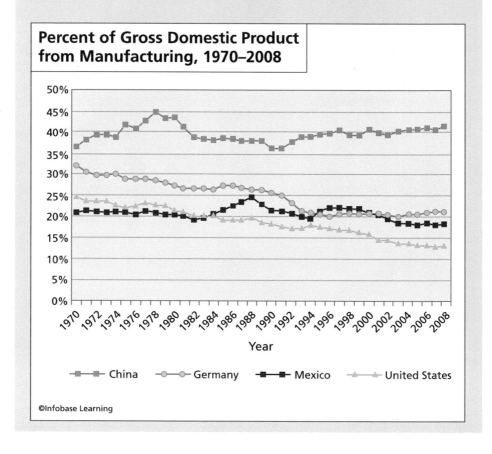

Percent of Gross Domestic Product from Manufacturing, 1970–2008

©Infobase Learning

contrast, many less developed countries continue to have economies that are dominated by manufacturing. In developed countries, the consumer goods we buy—televisions, cell phones, clothes, and other things—are imported from elsewhere. The consequence is that manufacturing has become a much smaller part of our economy today.

Many people now refer to developed countries as "postindustrial societies" that operate via "knowledge economies" or "service economies." People in these postindustrial societies arc lcss likcly to make their livings by growing crops or by producing things, like cars and clothing. Instead they work in industries that provide services to others or create and manage information and technology. **Service industries** include restaurants and health care facilities, while **knowledge industries** include education and the media. Most of the fastest-growing jobs in the United States fall into these categories, especially jobs in health care and in computer technology. Some argue that we have moved past the service economy phase, as more and more service jobs are outsourced or mechanized. **Outsourcing** occurs when companies shift work to another organization, often one located in a different country. For instance, when you have a computer glitch and call customer service, you are often connected to a representative in India or Ireland; some cities have their parking tickets processed by clerks in Africa; and even x-rays are often read by radiologists around the world. **Mechanization** means that jobs formerly performed by human workers are replaced by technology. For instance, you can use the ATM instead of handing your check to a bank teller, and "customer service" increasingly means prerecorded messages that have replaced human representatives. IBM, for example, has been working on a computer called Watson. Watson has been programmed to play Jeopardy; the intent here is to expand his question-answering skills to enable Watson to be a useful replacement for human workers. Such innovations strongly suggest that our economy is currently in a transition period, and we will have to wait and see where social change takes us next.

Through examining the changes in our economy, we can see that technology has had a substantial effect on society. It has replaced workers, changed the organization of our work (and nonwork) lives, and resulted in entirely new ways of life. But technological change, while it can enhance and facilitate much of what we do, may also be responsible for increasing inequality in society. Not everyone has access to the same technological resources, and good jobs in our economy require new (and sometimes very extensive) knowledge. Keeping up with new technology is also expensive. In 2010, someone in the United States who wanted to maintain a fast Internet connection and an Internet-enabled cell phone easily spent over $100 a month to do so, a sum out of reach of many poor and working-class families. In addition, jobs requiring physical labor or skill have been taken over by technology or outsourced, so those without advanced educational credentials and technological skill are often stuck in the worst (and worst-paying) jobs.

Despite some fairly visible signs, many people are not aware of this increase in economic inequality. One of the major reasons for this is because less money now buys more consumer goods—especially technological goods—than it used to. Thus, despite the fact that Internet service is expensive, it was not even available a generation ago. Most middle-class and many working-class families own cell phones, computers, televisions, DVD players, washing machines, dishwashers, microwaves, and other technological devices that their parents could not afford, and thus people feel richer in absolute terms even when they have less in relative terms. This example highlights the fact that any given social change is neither entirely good or entirely bad. Instead, most social changes are a mixed blessing (or a mixed curse) with many complex effects on society and on individuals.

Further Reading

Bell, Daniel. *The Coming of Post-Industrial Society*. New York: Harper Colophon Books, 1974.

Gilbreth, Frank B., Jr., and Ernestine Gilbreth Carey. *Cheaper by the Dozen*. New York: HarperCollins Publishers, 2005.

Hounshell, David A. *From the American System to Mass Production, 1800–1932: The Development of Manufacturing Technology in the United States*. Baltimore, Md.: Johns Hopkins University Press, 1984.

Kanellos, Michael. "Perspective: Myths of Moore's Law." CNET News. http://news.cnet.com/Myths-of-Moores-Law/2010-1071_3-1014887.html (accessed July 11, 2010).

Marx, Karl, and Friedrich Engels. "Wage Labour and Capital." Marxists Internet Archive Library. http://www.marxists.org/archive/marx/works/1847/wage-labour/index.htm (accessed July 9, 2010).

Ritzer, George. *The McDonaldization of Society*. 5th ed. Thousand Oaks, Calif.: Pine Forge Press, 2008.

Smelser, Neil. *Social Change in the Industrial Revolution: An Application of Theory to the British Cotton Industry*. Chicago: University of Chicago Press, 1959.

Smith, Adam. An *Inquiry into the Nature and Causes of the Wealth of Nations*. London: Methuen & Co., 1904.

Taylor, Frederick W. *The Principles of Scientific Management*. New York: Norton, 1967.

Thompson, Clive. "What is I.B.M.'s Watson?" *New York Times*, June 14, 2010, MM30.

Timmerman, Kelsey. *Where am I Wearing? A Global Tour to the Countries, Factories, and People that Make Our Clothes*. Malden, Mass.: Wiley, 2008.

Weber, Max. "Bureaucracy," in *From Max Weber: Essays in Sociology*, edited by H.H. Gerth and C. Wright Mills, 196–244. London: Routledge, 1948.

CHAPTER 4

GLOBALIZATION

Let's say you have just moved into a new apartment and need to buy some furniture. You head down to the store, where you buy a desk with a wooden top and aluminum legs. The metal for your desk might have been mined in Guinea, West Africa, and refined in Ghana while the wood was harvested and processed in Poland. Then the materials might have been assembled and packaged in China before being shipped on a boat from Panama, which runs on fuel from Saudi Arabia, to the United States. When you pay, the profits from the transaction might find their way back to corporate headquarters in Sweden. This long and complicated story is just one example of the process we call **globalization**.

Globalization refers to the process whereby different countries, economies, and societies become increasingly interconnected on a global basis and whereby people increasingly develop an understanding of themselves as part of the world as a whole. In his book *The McDonaldization of Society*, George Ritzer defines globalization as "the worldwide diffusion of practices, expansion of relations across continents, organization of social life on a global scale, and growth of a shared global consciousness." Let's take that definition apart. First, Ritzer mentions the fact that practices, or things that we do, spread from one place to every place. For instance, we can now find spaghetti, tacos, or stir-fry all around the world; movies and music produced in the United States play in Africa (and vice versa); soccer, baseball, and other sports are played in many countries; and world religions like Judaism, Christianity, Islam, and Buddhism have followers on every continent.

Modern furniture in a luxury condominium development in Washington, D.C. The materials used to build these pieces probably originated from various countries and traveled thousands of miles on its way to this condo. *(Wikipedia)*

Second, Ritzer argues that the connections between people and between governments now stretch across the globe. Throughout most of human history, people would have generally known only those living nearby, and governments would forge alliances only with neighboring nations. Even in the 1800s it was not uncommon for a person to live his or her entire live within a 10 mile radius, even in developed countries like the United States. Today, in contrast, countries on opposite sides of the globe can build alliances and people can build personal

Countries with McDonald's Locations, January 2010

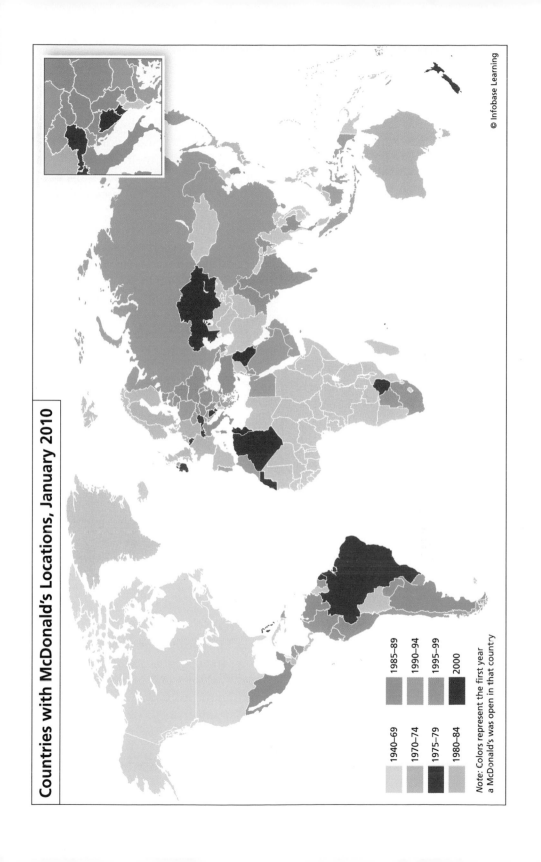

1940–69
1970–74
1975–79
1980–84
1985–89
1990–94
1995–99
2000

Note: Colors represent the first year a McDonald's was open in that country

© Infobase Learning

or business relationships with others all around the world. These connections are facilitated by Ritzer's third point, the fact that we have developed new ways of organizing our social life that both enable and are enabled by globalization. So, for instance, grandparents who live far from their grandchildren can use technologies like Skype and videoconferencing to watch their grandchildren grow up. And stockbrokers in New York City might have to start work at 4 a.m. because that is when the markets open (because of the different time zones) in the United Kingdom.

Finally, Ritzer argues that globalization involves the development of a global consciousness. In other words, we now see ourselves as part of a global world and are conscious of the interconnections between people and between nations. As we have seen in the global economic crisis that began in 2008, economic problems in one nation easily spread to others; similarly, environmental problems created in one part of the globe can affect everyone. Indeed, the World Values Survey, a global public opinion survey conducted between 2005 and 2007, found that 78 percent of people surveyed strongly agreed or agreed with the statement "I see myself as a global citizen."

The process of globalization began in the 1500s and 1600s as Europe first explored and then colonized areas in the Western and Southern Hemispheres. However, the speed and extent of globalization was intensified by new technologies developed during the Industrial Revolution, particularly the steam engine (which enabled ships to cross the oceans at much greater speeds) and transoceanic telephone and telegraph service. These new technologies, which were expanded and enhanced during the 1800s, allowed people in distant parts of the world to meet each other, learn about each other's cultural practices, and develop long-distance business and family relationships. Today, the effects of globalization reach almost everyone in the world—they have reshaped our work and education opportunities, the products and services we buy, the forms of cultural expression we have access to, and many other aspects of how we live our lives. Globalization is thus a major form of social change in the contemporary world.

THE CONSEQUENCES OF GLOBALIZATION

Like changes in technology, globalization has both positive and negative effects on individuals and on societies. On the one hand, globalization has significantly expanded many people's access to technologies and opportunities that they might not have been able to participate in if the world were less globalized. For instance, medicines developed in European universities to treat tropical diseases can now be made available to people suffering from those diseases in small villages in Africa. Poor students in Chile can visit an Internet café to learn about life in other countries. People in Estonia whose parents grew up without telephone service can now easily afford two separate cell phones, one for work and one for social and family life, and thus stay in touch with relatives and friends across Europe. And individuals all around the world can move to other countries to pursue jobs and educational opportunities. In 2008, for example, nearly 10 percent of all adult Filipinos were working abroad, while almost 700,000 international students were enrolled in colleges and universities in the United States (45 percent of these were from India and China combined).

But despite these many benefits, globalization is not all good. Most importantly, the benefits of globalization are not available to everyone. Even though the lives of some poor people have been improved by access to medical technologies, educational opportunities, and other benefits of globalization, these opportunities and amenities are out of reach for many people. For instance, the average citizen of Niger lives on $700 U.S. dollars a year—certainly not enough to enable that citizen to buy time in an Internet café, pay for good medicine, or send a child to study in the United States.

But the inequality globalization maintains is not limited to individuals. Globalization can also increase the degree of global inequality by exploiting the resources of some for the benefit of others on a much broader scale. Drug companies from the United States and Japan, for example, have sought to patent plants found in the Brazilian rainforest and keep the profits for themselves rather than having those profits remain in the hands of the people who live with and use these plants or even the country in which the plants are found and harvested. On the other hand, the outsourcing of manufacturing and customer service jobs from the United States to less developed countries has left workers in the United States unemployed while providing new sources of income elsewhere.

Another of globalization's effects has been the increased likelihood of global military conflicts. Instead of fighting over the exact location of their borders, countries now fight for global power and to gain or keep control of resources like oil and water. A conflict in this age of globalization can involve soldiers from dozens of nations fighting in several different parts of the globe. Globalization may also be responsible for widespread environmental and health degradation. The pollution caused by an oil spill in the Gulf of Mexico or by the burning of coal in power plants in China can spread to distant countries, causing harm to animals, to ecosystems, and to humans. Additionally, the spread of Western lifestyle habits—particularly diets high in fat, sugar, animal products, and fast food, and low in whole grains and vegetables—is considered to be responsible for increased rates of cancer in many other parts of the world. Finally, globalization has been responsible for the extinction of many local traditions, cultures, and languages around the world. According to Ranka Bjeljac-Babic, a linguistic psychologist, Europe's colonization process led to the extinction of at least 15 percent of all languages spoken at the time; today, approximately ten languages die out each year. The loss of linguistic and cultural diversity is not just the loss of a particular heritage and way of life—it also endangers our knowledge of

Changes in Life Expectancy in the Late 20th Century

Although the average life span people can expect has gone up all around the world, the gains have been much greater in some places than in others. One ironic fact related to life span is that wealth does not necessarily result in longevity whereas poverty and deprivation do contribute to early mortality. In some more developed countries, for example, pollution, diet, and other factors have begun to lower life expectancies. In Africa, famines, the AIDS epidemic, and civil war have contributed to a life expectancy that remains much lower than that in the rest of the world. While the continuing globalization of access to medical care is likely to increase life expectancy for some, pollution, war, unequal access to resources, and unhealthy habits very well might decrease it for others.

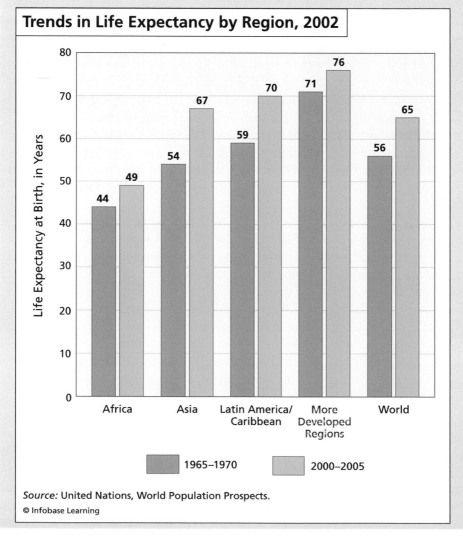

Trends in Life Expectancy by Region, 2002

Life Expectancy at Birth, in Years

Region	1965–1970	2000–2005
Africa	44	49
Asia	54	67
Latin America/Caribbean	59	70
More Developed Regions	71	76
World	56	65

■ 1965–1970   ■ 2000–2005

Source: United Nations, World Population Prospects.

© Infobase Learning

plant and animal species, our understanding of human history, and imaginative possibilities for the future.

Globalization is not a one-way process that spreads ideas and practices from developed countries to less developed ones. On the contrary, it involves the spread of a wide variety of ideas and practices with roots in many parts of the globe. Islam, for example, spread to Southeast Asia, some parts of Africa, and the Americas only after the age of globalization began. Benjamin Barber, in his book *Jihad vs. McWorld*, points to the spread of religious fundamentalism—not only Islamic fundamentalism, but also other sorts of religious and nationalist fundamentalism—as one of the key attributes of our current globalized world. Barber believes that we are currently experiencing a global conflict between fundamentalism and what he calls "McWorld." **McWorld** is characterized by a focus on efficient, capitalist markets; our global interdependence on other nations for resources; growth in information technology; and the inequalities created by global environmental damage. In McWorld, people see each other as members of a common global community committed to development and innovation. In contrast, **fundamentalism** is dedicated to protecting a particular cultural or religious identity, set of practices, and way of life—typically one rooted in tradition and custom. It is clear why fundamentalism and the McWorld view of life would come into conflict with one another, and by looking at recent armed conflicts around the world (like those in Afghanistan, Sri Lanka, and the Middle East) we can see that they do indeed come into conflict. The question is whether or not globalization is responsible for having created this conflict.

In fact, while the McWorld way of life was not possible before the emergence of globalization, fundamentalism has a long history as a feature of human societies. The term "fundamentalism" refers simply to a strict adherence to basic principles, whether of a religion, a culture, or something else. Most religions—and many other cultural groups—have had fundamentalist groups that have tried to encourage faithfulness to traditional practices and beliefs, and whenever such fundamentalism emerges, it gives rise to tension and conflicts between modernity and tradition. Globalization has played a significant role in the global spread of such conflicts, as fundamentalist groups are no longer confined to their own local geographic area but can broadcast their beliefs and their struggles around the world. But globalization in and of itself can not be held responsible for creating such conflicts. Indeed, it might be more fair to say that these conflicts developed because of the social changes associated with modernity and that globalization has simply made it easier for them to spread. Modernity and globalization are closely related, of course, but globalization might have been different had human history followed alternative paths.

MODERNITY
Many scholars divide the history of European civilization into three broad eras: **premodern society**, **feudal society**, and **modern society**. Some add a fourth era, **postmodern society**. These different eras of human history are distinguished by different sorts of social and economic arrangements. Globalization has been a key part of what has made modern society distinct but is not the only defining element.

Premodern Society
Ancient society was characterized by small societies governed by tradition and religion. There was not a significant role for individuals. Rather, people were part of tribal groups or families. Most groups survived either by practicing agriculture or by hunting and gathering, and leadership was determined either by tradition, the idea of **divine right** (where a deity is supposed to have appointed the leader) or by a contest of strength. Our knowledge of pre-modern societies begins roughly 5,000 years ago with the first written records—most historians define the period before humans began to write as **prehistory**. The first written records were written in Cuneiform script in approximately the 30th century B.C.E. It developed in the area we now call Iraq, which was one of the first regions to develop settled agriculture and permanent towns. Cuneiform documents were written with styluses on clay tables. While there are written records from many premodern societies, most people would have been illiterate and thus not left behind records of their own lives.

Many different periods and societies are included in what we think of as the premodern era. These include the Ancient Egyptian civilization that built the pyramids, the Iron Age, Ancient Greece and Rome, the Confucian era and many of the Chinese dynastic periods, early Christian civilization, the Mayans, the Incas, and the Aztecs, among others. Despite the fact that these civilizations are in our distant human past and had few literate people, they made significant advances in science and technology—plotting astronomical maps, developing ideas about medicine and illness, and building vast libraries. While each of these societies differed tremendously, all existed a long time ago. Scholars disagree about when the period we think of as premodern ended, but most put the end of this era between 500 and 800 C.E., pointing to events like the fall of the Roman Empire and the emergence of Islam as markers.

FEUDAL SOCIETY
In Europe, as the ancient period ebbed, society entered the **Dark Ages**. The Dark Ages were characterized by a loss of the knowledge gained during premodern times. In some parts of Europe, populations continued living in their traditional societies, but gradually the social arrangement known as **feudalism** replaced their earlier ways of life. The concept of feudalism is usually applied

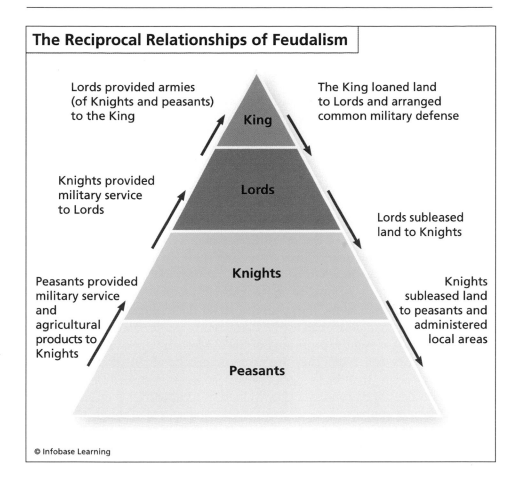

The Reciprocal Relationships of Feudalism

Lords provided armies
(of Knights and peasants)
to the King

The King loaned land
to Lords and arranged
common military defense

King

Knights provided
military service
to Lords

Lords

Lords subleased
land to Knights

Knights

Peasants provided
military service
and
agricultural
products to
Knights

Knights
subleased land
to peasants and
administered
local areas

Peasants

© Infobase Learning

only to European societies, though some other societies (such as Japan) had
similar systems. Feudalism began to emerge around the 700s with new political
constructs and regimes, such as the Holy Roman Empire.

Feudalism was an economic, social, and political system in which land was
owned by aristocrats and inhabited by common people, who were called serfs,
peasants, or vassals. Feudalism was also characterized by a system of reciprocal
obligation, in which those at lower levels of the social order owed labor or the
products of agricultural output to those at higher levels of the social order. In
exchange, those at higher levels of the social order provided land, protection,
and sometimes dispute-resolution services. The people who inhabited the land
were typically not free to come and go as they pleased but were tied to the land
that they occupied. Thus, during the feudal period there was little conception
of individual rights (especially for those at the bottom of the social order) and a
great emphasis on tradition and maintaining current ways of doing things. Fur-
thermore, because people were tied to the land, many never traveled far from
their homes or encountered other ways of doing things.

The Modern Period

In normal everyday speech, we use the term "modern" to refer to things that are new or contemporary, like "modern furniture" or "modern drama." But like many theoretical concepts, the idea of **modernity** has a particular meaning in social theory. When we talk about modernity in sociology, what we mean is not "now." Instead, modernity is a particular period of human civilization and social experience with a set of characteristics that distinguishes it from other periods.

The beginning of the modern era is generally considered to have coincided with the final decades of the European **Renaissance**, a period between the 14th and 17th centuries that was marked by massive change in intellectual and artistic cultures, including a return to classical learning, advances in artistic techniques, the development of the scientific method, and changes in education. By the end of the Renaissance period, leading thinkers had moved away from theory and philosophy based in religion and tradition and instead were writing about and researching rationality and science. These developments, as we will see, were important in laying the groundwork for the modern era.

Modernity, then, developed as the Renaissance period ended. Social theorists and historians peg the beginning of the modern era as occurring between the 17th century and 1900. They are no more precise about when modernity ended—some argue that the modern era came to a close between the 1960s and the 1980s as developed countries transitioned to a knowledge economy; others say that the current period is still part of the modern era. Though this might seem like a vague timeline, it is fairly precise in terms of the thousands of years of human history. Eras of civilization simply do not have defined start and end dates. And although modernity is generally thought to have arisen from within a European context, it is not a specifically Western phenomenon. It is closely related to the process of globalization, and thus one of the hallmarks of modernity is its global reach.

It must be emphasized, however, that modernity is not best defined by considering when and where it exists. Instead, modernity is identified by three main characteristics. The first of these is that things—especially technologies—change rapidly (Moore's law, discussed in the previous chapter, is a prime example of such rapid change). Second, the scope of change is global in reach and extent. This means that the social and technological change that is part of modernity occurs around the globe and that it touches all parts of life. Thus, instead of change occurring just in government and military technology, change affects our political, social, economic, and biological lives all at once. Finally, modernity brings with it a set of peculiarly modern social institutions. These include the commodification of goods and labor, the rise of the nation-state, and the development of inanimate power sources (in other words, power sources that do not rely on human or animal labor).

Commodification is a process through which goods and services become interchangeable, particularly because they are given a value in monetary terms. In the modern period, then, people sell goods and labor power in exchange for money, which they then use to purchase other goods and services. This contrasts with what occurred in earlier periods, when most people traded for goods and few worked for wages. A **nation-state** is an independent country whose citizens are entirely or predominantly of a single nationality or culture. European countries like France or Germany—at least before the massive increases in immigration that occurred after World War II—are examples of nation-states.

The rise of commodification is related to the development of capitalism, which expanded and intensified its hold on society during modernity. Both commodification and technological change were important for the Industrial Revolution, and thus the modern era was marked by an emphasis on industrial production. During the age of modernity, countries were also able to develop professional police and military forces, due in large part to the centralization of political control in nation-states and the commodification process that allowed police officers and soldiers to be paid cash wages. The Royal Exchange, a London facility in which traders were able meet in order to buy and sell goods, stocks, and other commodities, first opened in 1571; other similar facilities were opened in many European countries around the same time. Though one might assume that bureaucracy belongs in this list as well, bureaucracy (though somewhat different in form from what we are accustomed to) was already a social institution before modernity took hold. Bureaucracies, however, expanded considerably in modernity, both in size and in influence.

Several other important changes arising during the age of modernity must be included in this discussion. For one thing, modern era societies developed precise measures of time and space, including accurate clocks and standardized measurement scales. Clocks with pendulums that could keep time accurately were first developed in the late 1600s, and shortly afterward the minute and second hands were added. The mercury thermometer, allowing precise measurement of temperature, was developed in the early 1700s. And the standardized metric system of measures was first adopted in France in 1793. These developments were quite significant in altering social and technological relationships. They allowed trains to follow precise schedules, ships' captains to navigate accurately, and farmers to sell specified quantities of grain. In fact, the development of precise measures was even important for commodification, as it was not until weight scales were developed that currency could be standardized.

As modernity progressed, people became more likely to move away from the places in which they were born. These movements involved emigration to other countries and continents as well as migrations from rural areas and small towns to big cities. The consequence of these movements was the removal of social relations from locally specific contexts and networks; modernity gave rise to long-distance social relations as well as to relations with random strangers. The description of urbanization presented earlier in this volume discusses the consequences of these changes in more detail.

Finally, modernity involved and enabled the development of systematic knowledge about social life. The social sciences were key to the development of such knowledge. Indeed, sociology itself emerged with modernity in the same time and place and is actually a crucial part of the modern enterprise. Sociology, along with other social sciences, enables the collection of accurate data on human activities and behaviors. These data then enables governments, business people, and other actors to make better-informed decisions about how to proceed on a great number of things. Census data, for example, enable governments to decide where to build new schools; data on consumption patterns help business executives decide which products and how many of them to produce. Although some countries had collected census data on their populations long before the modern era (England, for instance, first collected household data in the Domesday Book of 1086), the practice of collecting census data spread rapidly in the 1700s and 1800s and remains a useful tool for contemporary societies.

Like all periods of social existence, modernity has had positive and negative implications for people's lives. The most important benefit of modernity has been increased security, particularly freedom from hunger and from disease. The technological and political developments of modernity have made it possible for agricultural production to increase, for sanitation and medical care to be improved, and for the products of these improvements to be more widely available. Most importantly, modernity has assured that products will be available at fairly stable prices and in fairly stable quantities.

But these beneficial aspects of modernity tell only half the story; indeed modernity is generally viewed as an unstable period. It has, for one thing, exposed humans to higher risks of many kinds. Modernity makes possible the risk of widespread environmental devastation. It allows for the possibility of technological global warfare, which includes the use of technologies such as those that created nuclear bombs that can destroy most life on earth. And it increases the possibility for political **totalitarianism**, a form of government in which there is an absolute dictator and no respect for individual rights or freedoms.

Modernity also brings with it a particular ideology, which is focused on making the world a "better" place. We might call this the ideology of progress. We can see the effects of this ideology all around us—in the decision to upgrade our cell phones as soon as a new model comes out, rather than keeping a perfectly good older model; in the rapidly changing opinions about the most up-to-date styles of clothing; in our greater trust for newly developed medicines and diets rather than traditional healing and eating patterns; and in our belief that scientific developments like DNA sequencing, deep-water oil drilling, and robotics will inevitably make the world a better place, regardless of the risks they might involve. As these examples show, progress undoubtedly brings many important developments that improve life dramatically for many people, but progress also brings many risks that can make life much worse—or that at least can cost a lot of money without bringing the sorts of improvements they promise.

Modernity and Surveillance

One additional practice that first developed in the modern era is **surveillance**. The term surveillance refers to the monitoring of people's behavior, activities, or information. Today, governments and businesses collect and monitor a vast array of data about our lives and activities, and they collect these data for assorted purposes. Credit card companies, for instance, build profiles of consumers based on what they buy and use this information to make decisions about whether consumers are good or bad credit risks. Charles Duhigg provides an interesting look at just how detailed such profiling can be: according to Duhigg, people who spend money on birdseed are good credit risks—after all, if they are responsible enough to care for wild birds, they will probably pay their bills on time—whereas people who frequent liquor stores and pawn shops are viewed as bad risks. Of course, once all of this information is available, it is possible for companies (and governments) to use it for other purposes besides credit profiling.

Surveillance is not only about the collection of data. It can also be about directly monitoring or observing a person's activities. The archetype of this type of surveillance was the **panopticon.** A circular prison designed by Jeremy Bentham, the panopticon made it possible for a centrally located observer to watch all of the prisoners without the prisoners being able to tell that they were being watched. Bentham first wrote about the panopticon in 1785; the design was widely adopted and became a staple of prison design in the years that followed. But the panopticon design has spread well beyond the prison walls. Today, many other facilities, including corporate offices and hospitals, use a similar design. In most hospital wards, for example, nursing staff are located in the center of a floor, with patient rooms arranged in a ring around this central nurses' station. Note that the doors to patients' room are almost always kept open.

The spirit of the panopticon is strongest however in applications that do not look very much like Bentham's design. One example of this is closed-circuit television cameras (CCTV), which permit surveillance from a distance and does not even require the presence of a human observer (at least not to perform the surveillance itself). A CCTV camera, sometimes concealed, can record the actions of people who are walking on public streets, visiting stores, or seated in college classrooms. In England, some of these CCTV cameras are connected to speakers; real-time images are monitored by police officers, who can scold pedestrians (also in real-time) for minor infractions like littering.

Surveillance cameras can also be embedded in computers or cell phones. In 2010, a Pennsylvania school district gave high school students laptops to take home, activated the cameras to observe what the students were doing outside of school, and then disciplined one student for what the school called "improper behavior" while he was at home. GPS tracking devices can also be used for surveillance. These devices can be placed under the bottom of a car without the owner's knowledge, thereby enabling police (or jealous spouses) to track the car's movements. At work, employers can use special software packages to track every keystroke employees make on their computers during the workday, thereby monitoring whether employees send personal emails or go e-shopping. These few examples are part of a much bigger picture.

Although some of these surveillance practices may seem excessive or unduly intrusive, most of us do not express much concern about surveillance. Indeed, many observers of social phenomena would argue that we eagerly embrace it. Hundreds of millions of Internet users post details about their daily lives to social networking Websites like Facebook and Twitter; many do not choose to enable the privacy protections available on such sites and thus make their personal information available to anyone on the Internet. Newer applications like Foursquare encourage cell phone users to check in at specific locations as they go about their day, enabling their friends to find them at the pizza store but also allowing thieves to know when houses might be unoccupied. Millions of people watch each episode of reality TV shows like Survivor, where (unpaid) contestants eagerly participate in a show that films their every move for weeks on end. These developments have led some to argue that we are currently experiencing "the death of privacy." In January 2010, for instance, Facebook founder Mark Zuckerberg told an audience that privacy was no longer a social norm.

As people become more and more comfortable sharing personal information for commercial and social purposes like Facebook, they also become more comfortable with government surveillance. In 2001, shortly after the terrorist attacks of 9/11, the U.S. Congress passed a law known as the USA PATRIOT Act. This law dramatically increased the power of law enforcement to engage in surveillance of telephone and Internet communication as well as to collect data on library patrons' reading habits, along with many other things. Though the powers of surveillance granted under this law are unprecedented in the United States, only 30 percent of people surveyed in a 2005 Gallup poll thought it went too far. In 2010 airports across the country deployed new x-ray screening devices that produce a fairly detailed image of what people look like underneath their clothes, exposing people to radiation while the image was made. A 2010 Gallup poll revealed that 78 percent of air travelers approved of these scanners. Both polls show that people in the United States have become accustomed to policies and practices that prior generations would have seen as an invasion of privacy.

Postmodernity

To some, the modern era is already over; to others, it is on its way out. Regardless of which group you agree with, the overarching question is "what comes after modernity"? The next period of social existence has come to be known as **postmodernity**. Postmodernity is a complex notion, but on the most basic level, in the postmodern era society is against the principles of modernity, particularly with respect to the modern era's emphasis on rationality and progress. After so many years of modernity, change has become the status quo, and this constant state of change makes the idea of progress irrelevant for understanding human social existence. This rejection of the ideals of modernity leads some observers of social life and norms to claim that postmodernity does not contain any ideals of its own, that it is simply a rebellion against what currently exists. But this is only part of the story; postmodernity is also defined by other characteristics.

For one thing, the postmodern era has seen the emergence of a new system of economic organization—**Late Capitalism.** The postmodern economy is defined by highly mobile labor, globalized markets and corporations, and mass consumption. Workers are no longer connected to one employer (or even one industry or country) for their entire careers, and employers feel free to hire and fire workers at will or to rely primarily on temporary and part-time workers. Companies exist beyond national borders, and indeed the global profits of some corporations now exceed the annual budgets of many countries. The same products are bought and sold all around the world. Perhaps most importantly, the postmodern economy is driven by the desire to purchase ever-greater quantities of goods and services, unlike the modern economy, which was driven by industrial production.

Postmodernity is also characterized by cultural changes. In the postmodern era, people are less accepting of authority and more willing to challenge the traditional order of things. At times, this translates into rebellion. Some observers of social phenomena associate specific movements (ranging from the student movements of the 1960s to the terrorism of today) with the rebellious spirit of postmodernism. Others, however, argue that the challenge to authority need not take the form of rebellion. Other trends related to this challenge to authority include drug use, individual production of media content (like blogs and home video), new cultural forms in music and video, and changes in personal lives like the increasing availability of divorce.

In general, postmodern society becomes more fragmented. We can longer easily pinpoint (much less label) something as "American culture" because our culture has become so diffuse and multifaceted that it can not fit neatly into the old definition. Think about television, for example. In the 1950s, there were three television networks that accounted for almost all of the television people watched in the United States. The programs offered on each network were fairly similar (some news, some comedy, some drama, something suitable for children, some advertising) and almost invariably reflected American mores and norms and lifestyles of the time. Today, despite the fact that six media companies own the majority of all television stations in the country, viewers can choose from hundreds of different stations, each one catering to a specific set of interests and identities.

Postmodernity is also marked by a decreasing focus on objective knowledge and truth. Instead of emphasizing scientific knowledge, the postmodern era allows each individual to determine what and whom they believe. On some levels, multiple different models of reality can coexist without people feeling any need to determine which is right.

The one major thing that does not change with the transition from modernity to postmodernity is the importance of globalization. If anything, globalization is even more important to the postmodern era because cultural forms, political action, and economic issues all take place on a global scale. A blogger in New York can collaborate with a blogger in Japan; their work can then be read by someone in Brazil. Labor activists in Mexico and the Philippines can work together on a campaign to improve working conditions for garment workers, while at the same time, the government officials charged with economic issues from dozens of countries can meet together to set common international monetary policy. Companies can easily move production and sales into new markets when it seems like a good deal, and economic conditions in China can affect local opportunities in Nigeria. These situations are all created by globalization, and whether we like it or not, the globalized world is here to stay.

Further Reading

Barber, Benjamin. *Jihad vs. McWorld*. New York: Random House, 1996.

Bauman, Zygmunt. *Modernity and Ambivalence*. Cambridge, UK: Polity Press, 1991.

Bentham, Jeremy. *The Panopticon Writings*. London: Verso, 1995.

Bjeljac-Babic, Ranka. "6,000 Languages: An Embattled Heritage." *The UNESCO Courier*, April 2000, 18–19.

Duhigg, Charles. "What Does Your Credit Card Company Know About You?" *The New York Times*, May 12, 2009, MM40.

Giddens, Anthony. *The Consequences of Modernity*. Stanford, Calif.: Stanford University Press, 1990.

Harvey, David. *The Condition of Postmodernity*. Malden, Mass.: Blackwell Publishing, 1990.

Lyon, David. *Surveillance Society: Monitoring Everyday Life*. Buckingham, UK: Open University Press, 2001.

Ritzer, George. *Globalization: A Basic Text*. Malden, Mass.: Wiley Blackwell, 2010.

Simmel, Georg. "The Stranger." In *The Sociology of Georg Simmel*, edited by Kurt H. Wolff, 402–408. New York: The Free Press, 1950.

Stiglitz, Joseph E. *Globalization and Its Discontents*. New York: W.W. Norton, 2003.

CHAPTER 5

COLLECTIVE BEHAVIOR

Collective behavior is any action undertaken by a group of people who are acting together, regardless of whether this action is planned or unplanned, coordinated or uncoordinated, goal-oriented or without goals. Collective behavior can also be called **collective action** or **herd behavior**. There are thus many different types of collective behavior, ranging from the uncoordinated action of a mob to a highly organized revolution. Collective behavior can be a response to social change, it can spur social change, and is sometimes not related to social change at all. This chapter and the two that follow consider three different broad categories of collective behavior. In this chapter, the focus is on less organized and coordinated forms of collective behavior, such as mobs, riots, fashions, fads, and panics; Chapter 6 considers organized collective behavior aimed at creating some form of social change; and Chapter 7 deals with collective behaviors like revolutions and terrorism, which are fundamentally designed to challenge the organization of society.

MOBS AND RIOTS

In March of 1991, a black man named Rodney King was speeding on a highway in California after spending the evening drinking and watching basketball at a friend's house. After police officers noticed King's car, they signaled to him that he should pull over. Because he did not want to face the legal consequences of driving under the influence of alcohol, King ignored the signals and did not pull over. After eight miles of pursuit—at speeds reaching

117 miles per hour—King's car was cornered. He and his two passengers were ordered out of the car. The passengers were taken into custody without incident, but the officers considered King's behavior upon exiting the car to be odd, thus leading the officers to fear that he was armed and dangerous (which he was not). The officers fired a Taser at King twice, then beat him with their batons and kicked him repeatedly, leaving him with many broken bones and organ damage. These acts of police brutality were captured on videotape by a private citizen. With the videotape as evidence, four officers were charged with use of excessive force and put on trial. A jury without a single black member did not convict any of them.

In the same month as King's beating, a 15-year-old black girl named Latasha Harlins was shot to death by a shopkeeper. Harlins had entered the store to buy a bottle of orange juice. She had money in her hand to pay for the juice, but she put the bottle in her backpack before approaching the checkout counter. The shopkeeper, a 51-year-old Korean immigrant woman named Soon Ja Du, did not see the money in Harlins's hand and shot Harlins in the back of the head with a handgun. While Du was found guilty of manslaughter (a crime with a 16-year prison term), the judge reduced the sentence to five years of probation, four hundred hours of community service, and a five hundred dollar fine.

These two events intensified feelings of injustice among poor black residents of Los Angeles. At the time of the trials, South Central Los Angeles was suffering from the effects of a recession that had left the neighborhood with a 14 percent unemployment rate; almost one-third of area residents lived below the poverty line and most felt that they did not have access to economic and educational opportunities or city services. Few businesses served poor inner-city neighborhoods, and those that did operate in such neighborhoods tended to be family businesses owned by Korean immigrants. Residents accused these shop owners of racism because of their high prices and their refusal to employ black workers (most employees of small immigrant-owned businesses tend to be family members). Thus, on the night that the King verdict was announced, tensions in Los Angeles were already at a breaking point.

Within hours of the announcement, violence broke out across the city. Crowds gathered at the courthouse, at police headquarters, and in the South Central neighborhood and began looting, destroying property, and attacking people. By the second day of the L.A. riots, gun battles were being fought between rioters and Korean shopkeepers and thousands of fires had been set, but law enforcement and fire personnel were slow to respond. The riots continued until military personnel arrived on the fourth day. By the time the rioting stopped, at least fifty-three people had died and about 2,000 had been injured; 3,600 fires had been set; 1,100 buildings and 10,000 businesses had been destroyed; and close to one billion dollars in property damage had occurred. Some areas of

South Central Los Angeles still bear the scars of the four-day incident. After the riots, the four officers were tried on federal civil rights charges; two officers were acquitted and two were convicted and sentenced to thirty months in prison.

To fully understand the sociology of the events described here, one must first understand the relevant vocabulary. The term **mob** refers to any disorderly crowd of people, and the term **riot** is used when this crowd begins to engage in acts of violence and/or property destruction. Mobs and riots are collective behavior events that occur without formal organization, when normal conventions governing social behavior fall away because of changes in circumstances. As the new circumstances emerge, new norms are created to fit these specific circumstances. Mobs and riots typically involve the spontaneous gathering of large numbers of people in a particular location in response to some sort of event. Often, this is because people experience distress when they compare their present situation to prior situations or in comparison to **reference groups** (groups to which people compare themselves). On occasion, mobs or riots can also emerge after nonstressful events.

It is clear how the elements of this framework apply to the L.A. riots discussed above. These riots involved large numbers of participants—estimates suggest hundreds of thousands of people took part, and of these, approximately 11,000 people were arrested. Normal conventions of behavior clearly broke down. Normal social life in cities in the United States does not involve gun battles between business owners and their customers, beating strangers, or setting fire to numerous buildings, but these actions became normal during the days of rioting. The riots developed in response to long-standing social problems in Los Angeles; it is, however, unlikely that they would have occurred had it not been for the Rodney King and Latasha Harlins verdicts—verdicts that created distressing comparisons in the minds of blacks living in Los Angeles. Yet despite the clear social issues that prompted the riots, the riots themselves were not organized or goal-oriented. Participants engaged in violence and property destruction because they were angry and frustrated and because it seemed like the thing to do at the time, not because of an organized plan to attract the attention of government and thus create social change.

The Los Angeles riots of 1992 are an example of a **race riot**. Dozens of race riots have occurred in the United States since the 1800s, as well as in other countries with significant racial inequality, but they were especially common in the late 1960s. It is important to note, however, that there are many other types of riots, provoked by varied circumstances and issues. One example is **food riots**, which are provoked by food shortages and often involve attacks against those who might have food or access to food sources. Another is **prison riots,** which pit prisoners against prison guards and administration. In 1971, about 1,000 prisoners (of 2,200 then incarcerated) in the Attica Correctional Facility in New York State rioted, taking 33 staff members hostage. Though prison-

Images of Riots

(clockwise, from top left): **Aftermath of riots in Athens, Greece in 2008.** *(Wikipedia);* **Riot in Algeria prompted by unemployment and the price of food in 2011.** *(Wikipedia);* **Anti-Chinese riot in Denver, Colorado, in 1880.** *(Library of Congress);* **Riot in Washington, D.C., after the assassination of Dr. Martin Luther King, Jr. in 1968.** *(Wikipedia);* **Riot in Moldova after the 2009 parliamentary elections.** *(Wikipedia);* **Riot in Philadelphia in 1844 in which anti-Catholic forces clashed with Irish residents.** *(Library of Congress)*

ers had long been unhappy with prison conditions, the riot was spurred by the death of black activist George Jackson, who had been shot by prison guards in California. Dozens of people—both prisoners and guards—were killed in the course of the riot.

Some examples of more recent riots include:

- The 2005 Cronulla riots, a series of race riots in Australia, sparked by violent scuffles between white and Middle Eastern youth on a beach outside of Sydney.
- The 3·14 riots, a series of riots in Tibet in 2008, that began when the police dispersed peaceful demonstrators who were commemorating the 49th anniversary of the Tibetan uprising against China.
- The 2007 unrest in the Val-d'Oise, a series of riots in French suburbs that were sparked by the deaths of two teenagers killed when their motorcycle collided with a police car.
- The 2008 Greek riots, which developed in response to the shooting of a 15-year-old student by two police officers.
- Food riots in 2007 and 2008 in Bangladesh, Burkina Faso, Cameroon, Cote d'Ivoire, Egypt, Haiti, India, Indonesia, Mozambique, Senegal, Somalia, Yemen, and other countries, in response to rising food prices.
- The 2005 riot in Toledo, Ohio, which was sparked by a planned neo-Nazi march.

But as noted above, not all riots occur in response to injustice or deprivation. **Sports riots**, for instance, can occur when spectators react after a game is over—and this can happen whether their team loses or wins! After the Boston Red Sox won the 2007 World Series against the Colorado Rockies, their second World Series title in four years, hundreds of fans poured into the streets to celebrate. These celebrations included setting a fire, flipping a truck on its side, and 37 arrests. Sports riots can even turn deadly. In 1985, before a soccer match between Liverpool, England, and Juventus of Italy, spectators began rioting in Heysel Stadium in Brussels, Belgium. When people tried to escape the mayhem, a concrete retaining wall collapsed, killing 39 and injuring 600. Despite the riot, the game was played as scheduled.

Unlike riots, mobs are not violent. Rather, they are large groups of people (sometimes called **crowds**) who happen to be in the same place and whose behavior becomes driven by the group. Groups in public tend to act in concert and in a similar way because of group dynamics. For instance, people watching a play, movie, or sports event are likely to cheer, applaud, laugh, or boo almost in unison. Mobs can occur in any sort of large-group situation, especially when something unexpected or unusual is happening. For example, when a blizzard shut down air traffic and supply chains at Kennedy Airport in New York City at the end of December in 2010, restaurants within the airport ran out of food. As a result, hungry, stranded passengers gathered in front of restaurants and began screaming at the staff. Similarly, mobs often form when people gather at government offices just before paperwork deadlines but find that there are insufficient staff to provide efficient service.

A more modern type of mob is the **flash mob**. Flash mobs are large groups of people who assemble suddenly in public spaces for a brief period and then disperse. Their activities, which often include some sort of choreographed but unusual and/or pointless action, are coordinated through text messages, social networking sites like Facebook or Twitter, emails, or other telecommunications technologies. The first flash mob was staged in 2003 in New York City by Bill Wasik, a magazine editor. Wasik sent dozens of people to Macy's, where they pretended to be shopping for a rug. Since then, flash mobs have become common events. People are drawn to participate for entertainment's sake, such as the flash mob that tried to stage a game of freeze-tag in a Wisconsin mall in December 2010; for social solidarity, like a flash mob of dancing teachers at a high school assembly in Washington State in December 2010; and for protest, such as a flash mob of students who blocked a London transit station for an hour in August 2010 in opposition to proposed changes in higher education financing in Great Britain.

FADS, MANIAS, AND PANICS
Though riots and mobs involve groups of people acting together in a particular space, collective behavior does not require that people be located in the same place. Fads, manias, and panics are all examples of such collective behavior. In each of these types of collective behavior, large numbers of people begin to think and act in similar ways. However, instead of involving the gathering of people in a specific place to respond to something, fads, manias, and panics involve the spread of an idea, innovation, or behavior through social networks. **Fads** are phenomena that become extremely popular for a short period of time. **Manias** are periods of excessive excitement. And **panics** are sudden, widespread fears. These phenomena were chronicled by Scottish writer Charles Mackay in his 1841 classic *Extraordinary Popular Delusions and the Madness of Crowds*. Mackay examined a wide variety of episodes of collective behavior, including investment schemes, fortune telling, the Crusades, hairstyles, and the myth of Robin Hood, concluding that people think and "go mad" in herds but return to sanity only as individuals.

Though today the word **fashion** is typically used to refer to current clothing trends, the term technically means "a prevailing custom or style" more broadly and is sometimes used to refer to fads. Fads cut across all areas of social and cultural life, from clothing styles to musical preferences, from food choices

Flash Mobs as a Form of Protest

People in the United States and many other democratic countries have the legal right to assemble publicly and protest against actions taken by their governments. Those same actions are illegal in many countries of the world with more authoritarian governments. Egypt, for example, had an Emergency Law in place continuously from 1981 through the 2011 Arab Spring, which limited rights of public assembly and protest and permitted authorities to arrest without charge or warrant those suspected of violating the law. This law allowed the government and law enforcement officials to ban street protest, political organizations, financial donations, public meetings, and even the production and dissemination of leaflets. In an attempt to get around these restrictions, Egyptian activists turned to the flash mob as a protest technique. Activists posted calls for participation on Facebook or used text messages to coordinate events, with explicit rules designed to conform to the requirements of the Emergency Law. For instance, a flash mob in June 2010 protested the torture and murder of Khalid Said by police; Said had posted a video of police officers dividing drugs seized in a bust amongst themselves. Participants dressed in black gathered at 6 p.m. and stood in silence, five meters apart from one another, facing the ocean. They then quickly dispersed—but not without taking video and photographs to post on Facebook. Such protests might have little effect in a big city in the United States, but in a society in which public assembly is highly restricted, they enable activists to be visible while lowering the risk of arrest and long prison terms.

to investment decisions, from cars to educational innovations. For instance, the Atkins Diet fad convinced participants to eat protein and fat and avoid carbohydrates, and the skinny jeans trend inspired ever-tighter denim until those jeans were turned into jeggings. But fads can also reflect and affect serious issues. For instance, starting in the 1950s, educators believed that the most effective way to teach children to read and write was **phonics**, an approach emphasizing the connection between sounds and letters. In the 1980s, a new approach caught on. Called the **whole language** approach, it focused on deriving word meanings from context. The whole language fad replaced phonics in many classrooms. Although educational researchers have found merit to both approaches, decisions about how to teach (like decisions about what to eat or what to wear) are often based as much or more on what is popular than on what works best.

Fads spread across a population through a process called **diffusion**. The diffusion of fads occurs when ideas or practices spread across **social networks**, with those individuals who are most similar or most closely connected likely to spread the idea or practice to each other, and with those ideas or practices

Fads by Decade

The website http://www.crazyfads.com is dedicated to archiving fads by decade, some of which are presented here. See how many of them you remember, and ask older friends and relatives about the fads they remember from their younger days.

1950s	1960s	1970s	1980s	1990s	2000s
Sock hops	Ed Sullivan	Star Wars	Legwarmers	Pokemon	Crocs
Elvis	Bouffants	Big Wheels	Neon	The Macarena	Uggs
Hula hoop	Tie-dye	Lava Lamps	Mullets	Tickle Me Elmo	Speed dating
Poodle skirts	Barbie dolls	Disco	Ouija boards	Grunge	iPods
Pez	Scully	Lite Brite	Pac-Man	The X-Files	High School Musical
Pompadours	Afros	Hot Pants	Rainbow Brite	Napster	Blogging
Beehives	Bellbottoms	Mad Libs	My Little Pony	Roller blades	American Idol
Saddle Shoes	Motown	Fondue	Transformers	Tamagotchi	Bratz dolls
Gumby	The Twist	Tang	Shoulder pads	Friends	Hannah Montana
Diners	Miniskirts	Holly Hobbie	Slap bracelets	Nirvana	Sudoku

that are seen as most successful being most likely to diffuse. Diffusion processes follow a particular timeline, represented as an S-shaped curve in which adoption of the fad is initially slow, progresses rapidly in the middle, and trails off at the end as only a few people committed to the particular fad remain. Scholars who are interested in the diffusion of fads use a technique called **network analysis** that lets them diagram the connections between people to see how a given fad spreads across networks of friends, acquaintances, and/or neighbors. Some people are **early adopters** who become part of the fad first. People who are close to these early adopters in a social network then adopt the fad too. A similar process of imitation occurs when ordinary people imitate celebrities or stars.

In a study of the practice of streaking on college campuses, Aguirre, Quarantelli, and Mendoza found that the likelihood of a streaking event increases under certain conditions: streaking events at other nearby colleges that are prestigious, degree of punishment inflicted on streakers, media coverage (particularly accurate media coverage) of past streaking events, and social and cultural diversity on campus. Research on fads like streaking shows that fads are not just odd behavior by irrational teenagers but are instead examples of complex collective behavior that can result in the development of new norms and social practices.

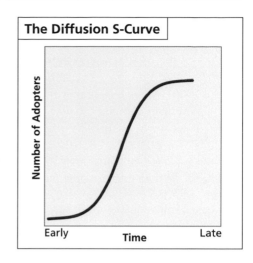

Companies interested in marketing their products to create fads capitalize on this idea of diffusion by using **viral marketing** techniques. Traditionally, this would occur through gatherings like Tupperware parties or simply by customers telling their friends about a given product. Today, however, with the popularity of social networking sites like Facebook and Twitter, companies aim to have customers become fans of the company or the product and share their enthusiasm for one or both with their friends. Social networking sites have been experimenting with applications and services that tell your friends what Websites you use and what products you buy (such as Facebook's short-lived Beacon system or the now-terminated Friends service on Netflix). Although these systems have not caught on, consumers do continue to tell their friends about products and services they like (often via email) and thus products spread across social networks and sometimes become fads.

Companies also seek to capitalize on the fact that people imitate celebrities and stars by hiring such individuals as spokespeople for their products. Thus, fads can be started intentionally by companies that pair their products with popular personalities. Of course, celebrities can popularize products and promote trends even without the involvement of the companies that produce those products. For example, the music group Insane Clown Posse uses a soda called Faygo in its performances, spraying the crowd with the drink. While the Faygo company does not support Insane Clown Posse (they prefer to be seen as a "family drink") the group continues to use and promote the soda, which is primarily available in and around the Insane Clown Posse's home state of Michigan. Because fans of the group want to imitate its practices and purchases, the Faygo company has found that whenever the Insane Clown Posse plays in a

(continues on page 88)

Tulipomania

One of the most classic examples of a mania is the Dutch tulip mania of the 1630s. Tulips originated in and around Turkey and were brought to Europe in the 1500s, where they rapidly became a desirable status symbol. Propagation of tulips requires care and can take a number of years, so the bulbs were expensive. However, it was not until the 1630s that speculators entered the market for tulip bulbs. The market for tulip bulbs peaked in February 1637, at which time a single bulb could sell for many times the annual income of a craftsman in Holland. During this period, many people purchased bulbs—or entered into contracts to do so—with the intention of reselling them at a profit. However, when the prices reached their highest point, buyers became less willing to pay a premium for the bulbs. At the same time, the government declared that people who had entered into contracts to purchase bulbs could exit their contracts by paying a 10 percent fine. As a result, purchasing contracts became unenforceable and prices dropped rapidly. Because purchasing contracts had not yet been fulfilled when the mania ended, few speculators lost much money—but several experienced major financial difficulties. In any case, the tulip mania has become a common reference point for people commenting on more contemporary episodes of financial mania.

Brueghal's painting, created just a few years after the tulip bubble burst in Holland, satirizes the frenzy over tulips by comparing tulip sellers, speculators, and buyers to monkeys. The painting hangs in the Frans Hals Museum in Haarlem, Holland.

Jan Brueghel the Younger's *Satire on Tulip Mania*, **c. 1640.** *(Jan Brueghel the Younger. Wikipedia)*

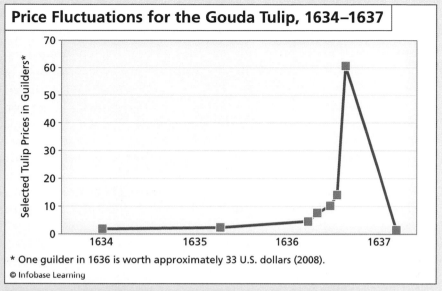

Price Fluctuations for the Gouda Tulip, 1634–1637

Selected Tulip Prices in Guilders*

70
60
50
40
30
20
10
0

1634   1635   1636   1637

* One guilder in 1636 is worth approximately 33 U.S. dollars (2008).

© Infobase Learning

The price of Gouda tulip bulbs before, during, and after Tulip Mania.

The chart above details fluctuations in the price of Gouda tulip bulbs over the period stretching from before to after the Tulip Mania according to data presented by Peter M. Garber in his article "Tulipmania" in the June 1989 issue of *The Journal of Political Economy.* Prices are presented in guilders, the Dutch currency. One guilder in 1636 is approximately 33 U.S. dollars (2008). Tulip purchases were measured by weight using a measure called the *aas*, which is approximately one-twentieth of a gram (or one-hundredth of an ounce). The picture below is a Gouda tulip from *Great Tulip Book* by an anonymous 17th century Dutch artist and is currently in the collection of the Norton Simon Museum in Pasadena, California.

Watercolor of the Semper Augustus tulip from the 17th century. *(Wikipedia)*

(continued from page 85)
new area, consumers call company headquarters asking whether Faygo is available in their area.

Manias sometimes begin as fads, but they go over the top. Allan Greenspan, the Chairman of the Federal Reserve from 1987 to 2006, coined the term "irrational exuberance" in December 1996 to describe what happens during a mania. Greenspan was describing the mania surrounding Internet stocks in the 1990s, but the term can be applied to any mania. Both fads and manias tend to be short-lived, and because of the extreme enthusiasm that is part of a mania, the end of the mania often has unpleasant consequences for those who have been part of it.

The financial crisis that began in 2008 was prompted in large part by a kind of economic mania called a **housing bubble** during which the prices of real estate increased rapidly and more and more people, including those who could not really afford to own property, rushed to purchase homes and other real estate. The frenzy of purchases reduced the availability of housing stock for purchase, which further increased prices through the laws of supply and demand. At the same time, real estate developers rushed to build more houses so they could profit from the boom in purchasing. Indeed, twice as many new single-family homes were sold in 2005 than in 1995. These purchases were aided and abetted by the **sub-prime mortgage industry**, which made loans available at high interest rates to borrowers who could not afford the payments. Ultimately, homeowners who were unable to make the payments lost their homes, adding more housing stock to the market just as purchasing slowed. Between 2007 and 2009, the average sales price of a new house in the United States fell by approximately 14 percent, marking an end to the housing bubble—and the home-buying mania.

The stock market has similarly experienced bubbles, such as the **dot-com bubble** in the late 1990s, which led Allan Greenspan to coin the term "irrational exuberance." Between 1999 and 2000 alone, stock prices doubled—but they soon fell rapidly, causing significant financial trauma to investors, retirees, and companies.

Financial bubbles are not the only type of manias. Manias can develop around products, music groups, or other things as well. For instance, the Beatles' world tour in 1963 unleashed a phenomenon known as Beatlemania in which frenzied fans became so infatuated with the music and the musicians that they could think of little else. Some observers of such social phenomena argue that 2010 was marked by iPad mania, as people rushed to buy iPads and iPad accessories, often without stopping to consider what role the iPad would play in their lives and whether it would work for them.

Panics are in some sense the opposite of manias. During a panic, people rapidly flee from some situation that has become troubling to them. Like manias, panics can be sparked by financial issues. Indeed, the end of the housing bubble can be viewed as a financial panic. While investment advisers counsel that the best strategy is to buy assets when they are inexpensive and sell them when they gain value, ordinary people have trouble following such advice. Therefore, the onset of economic difficulties and the beginning of a drop in asset prices often results in a collective sell-off in which prices drop much, much further—thus turning the end of a bubble into a massive panic.

The beginning of the Great Depression in 1929 in the United States involved such a panic—in this case, a **bank run**. As the stock market began to fall at the end of a bubble and banks began to call in loans that could not be repaid, people with money in those banks began to fear that the banks would fail and their money would be lost. Because federal deposit insurance had not yet been instituted, bank failures could have easily wiped people's life savings and many people rushed to the banks to withdraw their money. But the more people withdrew their money, the more likely the bank was to fail, and thus the bank run becomes a **self-fulfilling prophecy**.

Panics (like manias) are not always about financial issues. One kind of nonfinancial panic is **mass hysteria**, which occurs when large groups of people become ill or psychologically stressed due to circumstances that are entirely imaginary. For instance, if a room full of people mistakenly believe that they have been exposed to carbon monoxide, they may all believe that they have been poisoned and start exhibiting symptoms characteristic of such poisoning, like drowsiness. One of the best-known examples of mass hysteria occurred in 1938, when (in honor of Halloween) Orson Welles narrated a series of fictional news bulletins about an alien invasion of the United States on a radio drama show called *War of the Worlds*. Though Welles did tell listeners that the show had been fictional at the end of the broadcast, many had already stopped listening and hundreds of thousands of people believed that the alien invasion was real; some even reported sightings of UFOs during the broadcast.

Panics can also occur when fears develop in a specific enclosed location. These panics are called **escape panics**. During escape panics, people rush toward the exits, pushing and shoving their way through, ultimately creating a stampede. Often, some people fall down, a situation that always results in slowing the exodus and sometimes results in death. An escape panic at the Love Parade music festival in Germany in 2010 resulted in at least 19 deaths and 340 injuries when people got stuck in an entry tunnel.

Not all instances of collective behavior can be easily placed into one of the categories laid out here. For instance, consider **witch hunts**, which were common across Europe and North America in the 1500s and 1600s. During witch hunts, communities searched for individuals believed to engage in witchcraft, often women who were unpopular or who did not conform to social expectations. Individuals suspected of witchcraft would be put on trial, but witchcraft trials certainly did not conform to our modern standards of evidence and procedure. For instance, some witchcraft trials involved tying stones to a suspected witch and throwing her into a body of water. If she sank, she was innocent (though dead); if she floated, she was guilty—and thus was scheduled for execution as punishment for her crime. Scholars estimate that between 40,000 and 100,000 people were executed as witches in Early Modern Europe.

The best-known witch hunt in the United States occurred in Salem, Massachusetts from 1692 to 1693. Over 150 people were arrested, beginning with

(clockwise, from top left) "Witch No. 2" by George Walker depicts the Salem witchcraft trials, during which 14 women and five men (two victims shown in the pillory above) were put to death on the gallows; An accused witch proclaims her innocence in a print by George Walker. Many women accused of witchcraft had been engaged in commerce and property accumulation. The witchcraft hysteria that seized Salem in 1692 resulted in the death of 20 people. *(Library of Congress)* several women who were social outcasts and who were suspected of afflicting several young girls with epileptic fits. Of the 29 convicted of witchcraft, several were upstanding members of the community and religiously observant. Nineteen of those convicted were hanged, five of the accused died in prison, and one man who refused to enter a plea was crushed to death with stones. Today, people believe that the Salem witch trials were an example of mass hysteria, with people panicking, seeking someone to blame for their panic, and ultimately developing a mania for accusing and punishing suspected witches. Some people argue that the fits exhibited by the girls who started the hunt for witches in Salem were caused by a toxic fungus that grows on grain and leads to hallucinations, while others suggest that jealousy or a desire for attention spurred the accusations. The latter explanation is at the heart of Arthur Miller's play *The Crucible*.

Books like the *Harry Potter* series (which mentions the Salem Witches' Institute as the United States equivalent of Hogwarts school of wizardry) and Ann Meyers' 2009 book *Time of the Witches*; films like the 1996 version of Arthur Miller's play *The Crucible*; and television shows like *The Vampire Diaries* and *Charmed* all reference or are set during the Salem witch trials. But the real Salem witch trials became part of the cultural landscape of the United States soon after they began. In 1890, a jeweler from Salem even sold souvenir spoons based on the trials—and many artists made drawings, paintings, or woodcuts referencing them.

Witch hunts became much less common by the 1700s, and the last official trials and executions of suspected witches were in the 1780s in Europe. But modern witch hunts have continued unofficially in Africa and India, and there are still laws against witchcraft in Saudi Arabia and Cameroon. The phrase "witch hunt" is also used metaphorically in relation to any kind of mass hysteria and panicked process of accusing and searching out suspected immoral or politically suspect behavior. For example, Senator Joseph McCarthy and the House Un-American Activities Committee's persecutions of suspected Communists in the 1950s in the United States has often been called a witch hunt.

COLLECTIVE BEHAVIOR AND SOCIAL CHANGE

Unlike the types of social change described in Chapters 2, 3, and 4, collective behavior does not necessarily produce social change. Indeed, looking at mobs, fads, panics, and the other examples presented in this chapter, you might wonder why they are even relevant to a discussion of social change. Sometimes they are not—sometimes, people just act collectively with little explanation and little consequence. But often, collective behavior *is* closely related to social change. This relationship can extend in either of two directions, or in both at once. On the one hand, social change can spur collective behavior. On the other hand, collective behavior can spur social change.

How does social change spur collective behavior? Consider the L.A. riots. Although the events immediately precipitating the riots were specific criminal trials, their verdicts alone did not produce the riots. Rather, the riots stemmed from a combination of factors that had changed life for residents of South Central Los Angeles. The economy had declined. Unemployment had risen. Immigration and ethnic diversity in the neighborhood had increased, particularly among small-business owners. Life for blacks in South Central Los Angeles was not very good in 1992; in fact, it was worse than it had been a few years earlier. The "not guilty" verdict in the trial of the police officers who had assaulted Rodney King was the spark that ignited the kindling already gathered and ready to light. Other collective behaviors (like financial manias and panics) are prompted by changes in the structure of the economy, whereas fads may be produced by new technological developments.

Collective behavior can also spur social change. For instance, even though the L.A. riots did not incorporate specific demands for change, politicians and civic leaders realized during the riots that they would need to do something if they wanted to avoid such events in the future. Businesses and government invested in rebuilding damaged neighborhoods, and community activists worked to replace liquor stores with more socially desirable facilities like churches. These social changes might be minor in comparison to the changes that would have reduced poverty and unemployment among residents, but they were changes nonetheless. Similarly, after financial bubbles turn into panics, changes designed to prevent such events from occurring again in the future are often implemented. After the financial crises of 2008, several such changes affected how financial firms are regulated. However, since the goal of financial firms is to make as much money as possible, they are always looking for the next loophole that can drive a profit-making mania—thus, while the exact same bubble may not recur, it is likely that a different one will. Another example might concern escape panics. Scholars who have examined such panics have found that they are most likely where crowds bottleneck as they seek a single exit—researchers thus recommend redesigning facilities by building in multiple obvious exits and obstacles like thick columns that can serve to break up bottlenecks before people can get to exits.

Because collective behavior of the types discussed in this chapter is not organized and goal-oriented, its ability to produce social change remains limited. But other types of collective behavior are much more able to produce social change. This is most likely to occur when groups organize with the explicit aim of creating social change, a subject to be discussed in the next chapter.

Further Reading

Aguirre, B.E., E.L. Quarantelli, and Jorge L. Mendoza. "The Collective Behavior of Fads: The Characteristics, Effects, and Career of Streaking." *American Sociological Review*. 53:569–584, 1988.

Boyer, Paul S., and Stephen Nissenbaum. *Salem Possessed: The Social Origins of Witch-craft*. Cambridge, Mass.: Harvard University Press, 1974.

Dash, Mike. *Tulipomania: The Story of the World's Most Coveted Flower and the Extraordinary Passions It Aroused*. London: Phoenix, 2010.

Garber, Peter M. "Tulipmania." *The Journal of Political Economy*. 97:3, 535–560, 1989.

Gilje, Paul A. *Rioting in America*. Bloomington, Ind.: Indiana University Press, 1996.

Mackay, Charles. *Memoirs of Extraordinary Popular Delusions and the Madness of Crowds*, 2nd ed. London: Office of the National Illustrated Library, 1852. Available online at http://www.econlib.org/library/Mackay/macEx.html.

Penenberg, Adam L. *Viral Loop: From Facebook to Twitter, How Today's Smartest Businesses Grow Themselves*. New York: Hyperion, 2009.

Rogers, Everett M. *Diffusion of Innovations*, 4th ed. New York: The Free Press, 1995.

CHAPTER 6

SOCIAL MOVEMENTS

So far in this book, we have primarily been addressing social changes that no one in particular planned. Individuals may have played a major role in such changes, for example, Rodney King in the unfolding of the L.A. Riots or William Levitt in the development of suburbia. But no individual or group related to these two changes actually sat down and said "Let's have a riot so we can achieve property damage and racial equality" or "Suburbs would be a better way to live, so let's demand that populations develop in that way." And this, in essence, is what social movements do.

The term **social movement** refers to collective action taken by organized groups in pursuit of some common goal when these groups do not have access to institutionalized power. Let's unpack that definition. We already discussed collective action in the previous chapter but must emphasize here that it is an essential part of the definition of a social movement. Simply stated, one individual cannot be a social movement. In order for something to be a social movement, it must involve a group of people. The individuals in this group must be organized to some degree. If they are not organized, they are more a mob than a movement. Organization need not be complicated or extensive, but there should be some coordination among the people who participate in the social movement. Social movements must also have goals. These goals can be small, specific, and clearly defined—something like increasing the number of police patrols in a specific four-block area—or they can be big and vague, like decreasing social inequality. There is no limit on what kind of goals a social movement can have, but if a

Social Movements

It would be impossible to create a complete and accurate list of all social movements—there are far too many of them and they can be found everywhere. This alphabetical listing, therefore, is not an attempt to list every movement that ever existed. Instead, it is a partial list intended as an illustration of the kinds of social movements that have existed or currently exist in the world. If you want to find out more about any of these, search online or ask a librarian to help you learn how to find library resources on them.

abolition of slavery

American Indian

animal rights

anti-abortion

anti-apartheid

anti-consumerism

anti-globalization

anti-war

Asian American

Back-to-Africa

Black Power

Chiapas

Chicano

Christian family

civil rights

Dalit ("untouchables")

disability rights

environmental justice

environmental

gay rights

Know-nothings

fair trade

feminist

Free Tibet

human rights

immigrant rights

independence

indigenous peoples

Ku Klux Klan

labor

men's movement

militia

Moral Majority

nativism

nationalist

neurodiversity

nuclear non-proliferation

open-source software

pro-choice

pro-democracy

Prohibition (of alcohol)

same-sex marriage

slow food

straight edge

student movement

survivalism

Tea Party

women's suffrage

World Social Forum

Zapatista

group has no goals it is not a social movement. Finally, social movements are to some degree denied access to institutionalized power. In other words, they cannot get what they want simply by asking for it or deciding to make a change—if they were in power and could do such a thing, they would be engaging in reform (discussed in the next chapter) rather than participating in a social movement.

Aside from meeting these basic criteria, social movements are diverse in every way. They emerge in different places and times, have wildly different goals, have adherents who behave in very different ways, and produce a variety of different outcomes. The definition of social movements is broad enough to encompass movements as disparate as the Ku Klux Klan and the Civil Rights Movement; the global labor movement and the small-town movements for improved public services; the movement to abolish slavery in the early 1800s and the movement supporting gay rights in 2010. As this short list shows, social movements can and do have very different agendas. But despite these differences, researchers who study social movements can ask a common set of questions about them—questions that are also important to the activists who are part of social movements and the governments and other groups who wish to limit or prevent such movements.

The first set of questions we can ask address the overarching issue of how movements happen: when and how they arise, what they want, and who gets involved and why. Next we can ask what movements do: how they are organized, whom or what they are fighting against, what sorts of activities they engage in, and what sorts of claims they make. Finally, we can ask what about movement results: whether they achieve their goals, whether they have any other impact (good or bad) on society, and whether and how the government or their target(s) react to them.

HOW SOCIAL MOVEMENTS HAPPEN

For a social movement to accomplish anything, it must first get started. And in order for it to get started, there must be some problem or issue that the movement—and the people who will be part of it—want to address. The problems or issues that movements want to address are called **grievances**. Grievances may arise suddenly—for instance, if a government passes a new law that limits the rights of immigrants in a way that they were not previously limited, this would be a sudden new grievance that immigrants and their allies might want to mobilize against. Many grievances, however, do not arise suddenly but are long-lasting features of a society. For example, grievances might exist about racial or economic inequality, about tax rates, about the educational system, or about pollution being released from a nearby factory for years, decades, or even generations. At some point such grievances become the foundation of a social movement. What this means is that while grievances are a necessary element in the formation of a social movement, they are not the only thing criteria. Grievances can exist for many years without leading to a social movement forming. Only when other factors line up will a movement emerge.

Neil Smelser was one of the first sociologists to engage in a serious study of the formation of social movements. He, along with many other early scholars of social movements, believed that social movements were an irrational response to problems and that people with grievances who behaved rationally would find another way to solve them. Such a perspective, of course, leaves little room for understanding the power dynamics that affect social movements' access to power. But that shortcoming aside, Smelser did develop a five-step model for how social movements come into existence.

The first step is *structural conduciveness*, which means that collective action to address some situation is possible. Second, a *strain* must develop to prompt the social movement. This is where grievances fit in. Third, a general agreement must develop among potential movement participants that something must be done, something Smelser calls *generalized belief.* This third state is where Smelser's belief in the irrationality of movements is significant because Smelser argues that generalized belief is typically exaggerated and hysterical. Fourth, *mobilization* occurs, as leaders draw on generalized beliefs to encourage people to participate in the movement. The last stage, which is more a response to movements than part of the process that induces movement emergence, is *social control.* Social control refers to attempts by governments or other targets of social movement activism to limit or repress movement activity.

Contemporary scholars argue that Smelser's model and its emphasis on irrationality as the basis for social movement activism is not the best way to understand the dynamics of social movements. These scholars tend to argue that the level of grievances in the population stays fairly constant. Therefore, except when a new grievance is suddenly imposed, movements do not emerge on the basis of grievance development. Instead, they argue, movements emerge when other conditions change to make mobilization possible. One group of contemporary scholars advocates **resource mobilization** as a condition that makes movement formation possible. These scholars argue that when a potential movement has access to adequate resources, it will mobilize and begin pressing for change. Resources are often defined in economic terms, but there are many other types of important resources besides money, for example, skill, knowledge, time, and access to media. The feminist movement that began to emerge in the late 1960s illustrates this point. To begin with, feminist activists used political conferences and underground newspapers to recruit others to the cause. Moreover, the number of women who had leadership skills was increasing as the number of women involved in other social movements and among college students was steadily growing during the decade. Thus, though many women had had grievances about gender inequality for years prior to the emergence of the feminist movement, it may have been the availability of media, networking, and skill resources that enabled the feminist movement to emerge when it did.

Another set of potential explanations for when social movements emerge focuses on political environment. These explanations are based on the premise that grievances always exist but that movements emerge only when the political environment is right for them. When a particular political party gains power in the government after an election, it may be more open to the ideas or demands of a potential movement. Sensing that opening, a movement will mobilize where it otherwise would not have. One example that illustrates this concept is the Supreme Court decision in *Brown vs. Board of Education*, which ended legal racial segregation in public schools in the United States in 1954. This change weakened the regime of racial segregation in the U.S. South seem and thus encouraged the mobilization of the Civil Rights Movement.

Regardless of how a movement gets started, it cannot continue without mobilizing participants. Most people who support a movement will not become core participants or activists for that cause. For instance, after a ballot initiative repealed same-sex marriage in California in 2008, about 2,000 protesters gathered in the streets of San Francisco, a very low number when you consider that a poll on this issue showed that about 60 percent of people living in San Francisco were in favor of same-sex marriage rights. If all of the same-sex marriage supporters had come out onto the streets, more than 480,000 people would have been at the protest—even allowing for people who were sick, who had to work, who were out of town, or who had other obligations preventing them from joining the protest. The obvious question here is why they were not.

Economists who favor **rational choice theory**, a model of human behavior that predicts people will think through their options and choose the one which is most likely to benefit them, argue that people do not participate in social movements they believe in because they are **free riders**. Free riders are those who benefit from something without actually participating in the effort to get that thing. In other words, people who believe in a movement's goals assume that someone else will do the work, attend the protest, write the letter, and do whatever else it takes. They want the movement's goal to be achieved, but they believe this will occur even without their participation, and thus they do not participate. The free rider problem is particularly likely to occur when movements seek **collective goods**, or outcomes that benefit everyone regardless of whether they participate or not. An example of a collective good would be less pollution—everyone (those participating in the environmental movement as well as those not participating in the movement) would be able to breathe easier. The caveat here is that participants are needed—if everyone is a free rider and no one participates, nothing happens.

Rational choice theorists argue that movements can overcome the free rider problem by providing incentives for people to participate. For instance, a potential movement participant might come to a protest to get a free t-shirt, because there will be bands playing and it looks like fun, because it makes him or her look good to others, or because the protest is an opportunity to meet and make new friends. Such incentives can be important in mobilizing potential movement participants, but despite the claims of rational choice theorists, they are not the whole story. Some people become involved in movements simply because they care.

The process by which individuals become involved in movements that they care about, without any other sort of incentive for participation, is called **self-recruitment**. Self-recruitment often takes place when a person has experienced a **moral shock**, a sort of sudden emotional stimulus that makes the individual aware of a grievance he or she cannot simply ignore. For example, someone who watches a video about the treatment of animals on factory farms might experience a moral shock and that shock propels this individual to join the animal rights movement. Or someone might absent-mindedly click through the sex-offender registry and become energized to fight against the right of sex offenders to live near schools.

People are more likely to become active in social movements if they are **biographically available**. This applies specifically to people who are free of commitments, ties, and responsibilities that would make activism hard for them. In general, those who are the most biographically available are individuals who are too young to have established a settled life; who do not have children, spouses, or other family members they are responsible for; and who do not have work commitments they are unable to miss. Though increasing numbers of college students who work long hours and have family responsibilities are changing this demographic, college students of the 1960s and 1970s were typically seen as the most biographically available, and not coincidentally, were at the center of many of the social movements arising during those decades. But biographical availability is neither a pre-requisite for activism nor an absolute deterrent to activism. Single mothers, for example, can hardly be considered biographically available. And yet many single mothers join protests for better child care. Those with full-time jobs and many financial responsibilities participate in workplace strikes. People who are caregivers for critically ill relatives demand access to better health care services. The bottom line is that when an issue is important enough, people will find ways to get involved.

Though many people do become involved in social movements because of moral shocks, incentives, or simply because they care about an issue and have the time, networks play a decidedly critical role in mobilization. People are much more likely to join a movement when other people they know are already part of that movement. They will go to a protest because their friends are going, join a strike because their coworkers are striking, or participate in a boycott because their family members stopped buying a particular product to support some social movement. Some of the best evidence we have about the role of networks in the mobilization of movement participants comes from Doug McAdam's research on a movement called Freedom Summer. Freedom Summer was a summer-long project in 1964 during which black civil rights activists in the South brought white college students to Mississippi to help in voter registration drives and provide other needed services to the state's poor and disenfranchised black population. Students who wanted to participate in Freedom Summer had to fill out an application describing their past experiences and the reasons why they wanted to participate. McAdam drew on these application forms, which he found in an archive, to explain who became involved in the project, why they chose to participate, and how they were mobilized. He found that most potential participants chose to apply because other people they knew from school and prior activist involvements were also planning to participate. Thus, the decision to become involved in a social movement—like the movement itself—is collective.

WHAT SOCIAL MOVEMENTS DO

In order to achieve their goals, social movements choose targets, create organizations, develop decision-making processes, select strategies and tactics, and find ways of communicating their messages to targets, participants, and the general public. Different movements make very different choices about each of these things—depending on when and where they are active, who participates, and what sorts of goals they have.

Though it is possible for a social movement to occur without a formal organization, most movements do create **social movement organizations**, formal structures through which activism can be coordinated and decisions can be made. These organizations vary from small neighborhood coalitions to official, registered organizations with presidents and budgets (like the National Organization for Women or Greenpeace). The decision-making processes of social movement organizations also vary. Some social movement organizations choose leaders, whether through democratic elections or self-selection. These leaders, perhaps in association with a group of advisors, determine what sorts of actions and goals the movement will have. For example, after the Montgomery Bus Boycott (the event that made Rosa Parks famous), black civil rights activists from ten states met and formed the Southern Christian Leadership Conference, or SCLC. Martin Luther King, Jr., was elected president and Ralph Abernathy was elected vice president. King did not single-handedly make decisions about all SCLC actions, but until his assassination in 1968, he was a major force in determining what SCLC and the broader Civil Rights Movement would do.

Other social movement organizations choose a participatory democratic structure for decision making. In **participatory democracy**, leadership is deemphasized or may not exist at all. When leaders exist, they are there to provide day-to-day support to the organization and to help facilitate meetings, but their opinions about what to do are not given any more weight than anyone else's. Instead, decisions are made through a **deliberative process** where all members are able to say what they think. In some participatory democracies, decisions are made by a vote; in others, members deliberate until **consensus**, or a broad agreement about what to do, is reached. Francesca Poletta's book *Freedom Is an Endless Meeting* discusses the participatory decision-making process of a variety of social movement organizations; the title of the book is a not-so-tongue-in-cheek assessment of what often happens when movements choose participatory decision-making. However, this process does give movement participants a greater sense of ownership of and belonging to the movement.

Protests and Targets

Edward Walker, Andrew W. Martin, and John D. McCarthy, three social movements researchers, conducted a study of all protests reported in *The New York Times* between 1960 and 1990. While the dataset is obviously incomplete—not all social movements involve protests, not all protests (especially those that are smaller and farther from New York City) are likely to make it into the pages of *The New York Times,* and the time period is limited—it nonetheless enabled them to develop a basic idea of what kinds of movements have been part of the U.S. landscape. Walker and his collaborators were able to classify the 15,519 movements they found

Demonstration protesting an anti-abortion candidate at the Democratic National Convention in New York City in 1976. *(Library of Congress)*

across the 30-year time period they studied according to the type of target, the tactics used, whether violence was part of a given protest, and what sort of group initiated the protest. The table that follows outlines their findings. Numbers may not add up to 100 percent because of rounding.

Note: By "conventional" tactics, Walker and his colleagues mean activities like information distribution, petitions, lobbying, press conferences, and lawsuits, all activities that are not disruptive. By symbolic displays, they mean activities like vigils, ceremonies, and theatrical events. Withholding obligations refers to strikes and boycotts.

Each social movement has a **target** (or targets), typically people or organizations or institutions that movement participants perceive as the entity (or entities) responsible for their grievances or best able to make the changes the movement wants to see. For many social movements, the most important target is the government, whether national or local. Governments have the authority to make and change laws and to alter patterns of law enforcement, and many social movement goals center around such issues. For example, movements to prohibit alcohol, to legalize abortion, or to end racial profiling by police are most likely to target government. Movements that seek to change admissions policies or a school curriculum target educational institutions. Those interested

Target	Tactics Used	Other Factors	Initiating Group	Primary Issue
Government: 63%	Rally or demonstration: 31%	Violence used: 9%	Occupational group: 16%	Environmental or Anti-nuclear: 8%
Corporation: 18.5%	Symbolic displays: 3.5%	Property damage occurred: 5%	Women: 9%	Women's rights: 3%
Educational institution: 18%	Civil disobedience: 14%	Arrests occurred: 15%	Youth not primarily identified as students: 5%	Peace: 11.5%
	Withholding obligations: 16%	Protest was in New York City: 27%	Students: 29%	Educational issues: 11%
	Riots or attacks: 4.5%	Typical number of participants: 50–99	Political group: 6%	Social policy: 12%
	"Conventional" tactics: 31%	Movement organization involved: 44%	Religious group: 4%	Economic issues: 8.5%
			Racial or ethnic group, not already classified elsewhere: 31%	Black civil rights: 28.5%
				Anti-immigrant or anti-ethnic: 2%
				Other civil or human rights or civil liberties: 16%

in changing investment practices or employment practices target corporations or businesses. Movements with an interest in environmental concerns might target government and/or polluting corporations. Social movements might even target individuals if they want to change people's own practices and actions, for example by encouraging people to drive less, switch to energy-efficient light bulbs, stop eating meat, or become more religious.

To convince their target(s) to take the steps necessary to make movement goals a reality, movements need to choose **strategies** and **tactics**. In common usage, we tend to think of these two words as having a very similar meaning, but to social movement scholars they are actually quite different. Strategy refers to the overall plan that movements have for how to get to the goals they want, whereas tactics refer to specific types of actions that movements can take to implement those plans. When movements choose effective strategies, they will be more likely to get the outcomes they want. Although social movement scholars disagree about whether it is possible to tell which strategies will be most likely to generate desired outcomes for any particular movement, they agree that movements need to consider a variety of issues in designing good strategies. This includes an understanding of the type of target they have selected, how popular their goals are, the types of goals and decision-making the movement has chosen, the degree to which the target and public opinion are favorable to the movement, how much or little access the movement has to those with power, and the likelihood that activists will face threats from the police or others in power because of their involvement. In addition, strategic creativity is more likely to help movements make an impact, as targets have more trouble ignoring or deflecting the unexpected. Movements can be more strategically creative when they know a lot about the target and the area in which they are operating; when they can think about that knowledge in new ways; and when they are motivated, persistent, and willing to take risks. Marshall Ganz calls this **strategic capacity**, and it is more likely to develop in movements with a well-developed leadership, which have connections to the various people who are part of the movement; where decision-making processes are open, happen often, and result in clear decisions; where the movement is able to get resources from a variety of sources; and where leaders are held accountable for their actions. Within these overall strategies, movements choose specific tactics to use in specific places and at specific times.

In general, there are two types of tactics: those that are **assertive** and those that are **assimilative**. Assertive tactics are visible, disruptive, and challenging—things like sit-ins, demonstrations, occupying buildings, or even violence. Assimilative tactics are less visible, non-disruptive, and much less challenging, such as petition campaigns and lobbying. Of course, there are many tactics that fall somewhere in between, like boycotts or mass meetings. At any given time, social movements will choose their tactics from a broader **repertoire**, or group

Time, Place, and Tactics

Social movement tactics change and evolve over time and across space. The images here show some of the tactics used by various social movements in a variety of locations and time periods.

(clockwise, from top left) This early 20th-century painting depicts the Boston Tea Party of December 6, 1773. *(Library of Congress)*; Railway strike in Tiflis (Tiblisi), Georgia, in 1905. This photograph is from Stephen F. Jones's *Socialism in Georgian Colors: The European Road to Social Democracy, 1883–1917. (Wikipedia)*; Expulsion of abolitionists and African-Americans from a meeting in Boston. *(Library of Congress)*; Civil rights march on Washington, D.C. *(Library of Congress)*; Protest for human rights in Gaza and Lebanon. *(Jonathan McIntosh. Wikipedia)*; Sit-in staged in Italy to protest homophobia. *(Stefano Bolognini. Wikipedia)*

of tactics already known and used in a given time and place. Repertoires and the tactics common to them change over time. For instance, early in the 20th century, marches and pickets were a common movement tactic. The lunch counter sit-ins of the Civil Rights Movement in the 1960s began a period when sit-ins and the practice of occupying buildings were common. Today, movements draw on tactics like the flash mob, which involves sending participants text messages instructing them to show up briefly at a given location and then quickly leave. These changes occur through **tactical innovation**, as new tactics are developed and then adopted by a wider range of movements. Tactical innovation is particularly important in maintaining strategic creativity, as targets will adapt to certain tactics over time, thus making them ineffective. A major reason why the flash mob tactic has caught on is because many countries have made other forms of protest more difficult by requiring protesters to get permits in advance of their protest and through other means. For instance, in 2010, the U.S. Court of Appeals ruled that it was legal for public universities in Louisiana to require that demonstrators who are not university students submit their social security numbers at least one week in advance in order to get a permit to demonstrate. The flash mob avoids such impediments because it is unpredictable, temporary, and hard to trace.

Strategic choice, though, is not only about the selection of particular tactics to use at times when a social movement decides to take action. It is also about what social movements scholars call **framing**, or the ways in which movements explain themselves and their goals. Framing is used to communicate with the target, the media, the general public, allies, and movement membership. There are three main types of framing: **diagnostic** framing, which explains what the problem is that the movement is trying to solve and why it is a problem; **prognostic** framing, which proposes a solution to the problem, typically the goal that the movement is trying to achieve; and **motivational** framing, which encourages people to support the movement and become or stay active in it. Movements need to work hard to choose framing strategies that will communicate their messages clearly and get the attention they want without contradicting (or confusing) the core message, identity, or ideology of the movement. This can be very tricky as the example below illustrates.

Malcolm X, a leader in the Black Power movement, said that blacks should fight for respect and equality "by any means necessary." That statement was a powerful framing technique for the Black Power movement. It drew on all three of the framing techniques described above because it identified a problem, specified a goal, and provided motivation to potential movement participants by demonstrating the dedication the movement had to its cause. The same phrase, however, would have been far less effective if it were used by an anti-war movement. Why? Primarily because many anti-war activists are pacifists who do not believe in violence, and "by any means necessary" suggests that violence might be used. This framing strategy would have led to disagreements within the movement and a loss of support from many activists.

The most successful framing strategies tend to be those that are powerful, that resonate with activists and potential supporters, and that are memorable. One movement that recognized this concept was the AIDS Coalition to Unleash Power, better known as ACT UP. Formed in 1987, ACT UP was a coalition engaged in political action that encouraged more research into AIDS and better access to AIDS treatment. Because people in the 1980s associated AIDS with gay men and with IV drug users, both stigmatized and socially unpopular groups, ACT UP had to work hard to get people to pay attention to and care about their message. One of ACT UP's most famous framing strategies was the slogan "SILENCE = DEATH," which they printed on posters with pink triangles (a symbol used to identify gay men in Nazi concentration camps) and held up at a demonstration in front of the largest post office in New York City on the night when tax returns were due, guaranteeing themselves media coverage. Other framing strategies ACT UP used including distributing condoms along with instructions about safe sex; holding die-ins (protests where activists pretended to die), including one in St. Patrick's Cathedral in New York City to protest the Catholic Church's doctrines about sex education and condom use; and hanging a giant banner over the timetable at New York City's Grand Central Station that read "One AIDS death every 8 minutes." Although ACT UP certainly did not achieve all of its goals—there is still no cure for AIDS and treatment remains very expensive—it certainly achieved some of them, and this is probably due in large part to the impact of their framing strategies and media savvy. Today, there is funding for AIDS research and for AIDS treatment and most people are aware that AIDS affects people of all kinds, including heterosexual women who do not use drugs.

THE CONSEQUENCES OF SOCIAL MOVEMENTS

Most people participate in social movements because they want to change something, and this raises one of the most important questions about social movements—what it takes for them to achieve their goals. Social movements, of course, have many different kinds of goals, and there are just as many ways of achieving them. Goals may be achieved through governmental action, like the passage of new laws or favorable court decisions. They may be achieved by changes in an organization's policies or procedures. Or they may be achieved through new kinds of knowledge or changes in culture or personal practices.

One of the most difficult aspects of studying the impacts of social movements is figuring out how to measure those impacts. Traditionally, scholars of social movements considered movements successful only if they achieved everything they wanted, a difficult and unlikely prospect. Consider the gay rights movement in the United States: it is far from achieving everything it wants. On the other hand, anyone who knows something about the movement is likely to agree that it has made an enormous impact on society. Forty years ago, same-sex sexual activity was illegal in most places in the United States; people could even be arrested just for wearing clothes traditionally associated with the other sex. Very few people could be open about being gay or lesbian and expect to keep their jobs, particularly if they worked in education, health care, or government, and gay and lesbian people feared for their lives and safety if strangers found out about their sexual orientation. Homosexuality was even defined as a mental illness for which people could be locked in mental hospitals against their will! Today, about 20 U.S. states prohibit employment discrimination on the basis of sexual orientation; six permit same-sex marriage. Homosexuality was removed from the list of mental illnesses in 1986, and prohibitions on same-sex sexual activity were struck down by the U.S. Supreme Court in 2003. There are gay and lesbian athletes, movie stars, musicians, and politicians—not to mention teachers and doctors—who are able to do well in their respective careers. Gay rights activists today are still fighting to end hate crimes against gays and lesbians, to expand access to marriage rights and to anti-discrimination protection, and to increase social acceptance, but they have achieved many of the things that activists in the 1960s only dreamed of.

Considering movements like the gay rights movement helped social movements scholars—and activists—move away from the limited framework that focused only on success or failure. Today, we can understand that movements have various impacts and outcomes that can include reaching some goals while falling short of others. This expanded perspective has also allowed us to understand that movements can have unintended consequences. These unintended results can include entirely accidental bonuses to sought-after goals. Alternatively, they can be the opposite of what movements wanted. For instance, the temperance movement, which is the movement that pushed for the prohibition of alcohol and eventually won a constitutional amendment in 1919 that banned alcohol (at least until it was repealed in 1933), had a number of unintended consequences. In the absence of store-bought liquor, some people turned to methyl alcohol, a kind of alcohol distilled from wood that is highly toxic and can causes blindness or death. Ironically, this practice led to the creation of the cocktail—because methyl alcohol does not taste very good, people began to mix it with juices, sodas, or sugar to make it taste better. Other unintended results were more serious. Underground and illegal producers of alcohol, who often had connections to organized crime, became very rich during Prohibition. Prohibition also led to a significant decrease in federal tax revenues because the government could no longer tax what it had made illegal to sell. In a rather odd twist to this, some people believe that the federal income tax was expanded as a way to make up for this decline in tax revenues, thus arguing that the federal income tax was an unintended consequence of the temperance movement!

A key unintended consequence of many social movements is the rise of **countermovements,** which are social movements that emerge in response to another movement with the specific purpose of pushing for opposing goals. Countermovements tend to arise when the movements they oppose have achieved some impacts but not yet decisive ones, and they use framing strategies that directly reference the original movement. Movements and countermovements often engage in direct conflict with one another, holding counterdemonstrations at each other's events, creating media campaigns against each other, or tying each other up in legal battles. In fact, these activities give countermovements a tactical advantages, as they can use such activities to force the movements they oppose to focus their energy on the countermovement rather than on achieving their intended goals. On the other hand, movements can also use countermovements to increase their own credibility and thus their impacts. For instance, during the Civil Rights Movement, pro-segregationist forces worked against civil rights activists by violently attacking them and by starting private all-white schools. Instead of limiting the impact of the Civil Rights Movement, though, these actions on the part of segregationists convinced many who had been uninvolved in civil rights activism to support the Civil Rights Movement and ultimately helped pass the laws that civil rights activists fought for.

Other examples of ongoing movement versus countermovement clashes center on contrasting views about issues like abortion and immigration. When abortion rights activists won a favorable court ruling in *Roe v. Wade* that legalized abortion, this encouraged the mobilization of anti-abortion activists. Anti-immigration activists encourage laws restricting immigration and new law enforcement crackdowns on illegal immigrants, prompting demonstrations and protest from immigrants' rights groups. And there are many similar examples of this phenomenon.

Regardless of whether we are talking about the intended or the unintended outcomes of social movements, scholars and activists are eager to understand what conditions make impacts more likely to occur. This question is a source of great debate among those who study social movements, and those engaged in the debate have proposed many diverse opinions and explanations. Some, for instance, suggest that movements with access to the most resources are likely to have the greatest impact on society. Others assert that impacts and outcomes are determined by the number of people who support the movement, along with their unity and commitment to the cause. Choosing good strategies probably has something to do with it, as does the degree to which political figures or movement targets are sympathetic to and accessible by the movement. Edwin Amenta, who studies movements that target the government, argues that movements are most likely to have an impact when they choose strategies that match the political environment in which they find themselves. But how to match strategy to context most effectively is another question, one that many scholars and activists continue to struggle to answer.

Tactical Innovation and the Pace of Insurgency

The graph below was created from data presented in Doug McAdam's article "Tactical Innovation and the Pace of Insurgency." McAdam studied the tactics used by black civil rights activists and how they related to actions taken by segregationists who wanted to stop the movement as well as actions taken by the government, which was the target of the movement. McAdam shows the Civil Rights Movement was continually revising and changing its tactics. Whenever a tactic caught on—be it sit-ins, Freedom Rides (bus rides where whites and blacks rode together on integrated buses in violation of state law), community-wide protest campaigns, or riots—segregationists and the government adopted new ways to counter that tactic. Therefore, the movement needed to move on to another new tactic. The graph further shows that when movement activity peaked, it prompted an increase in activity by the segregationists, who could then be understood as a countermovement that in turn prompted government action. Ultimately, the Civil Rights Movement began to make more of an impact when it figured out this cause-and-effect formula and chose those tactics that were most likely to prompt a segregationist response—something best accomplished by the Freedom Rides. In the context of sociological constructs, this story is an example of strategic creativity.

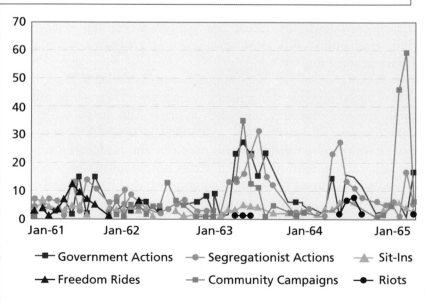

Movement, Segregationist and Government Actions in the Civil Rights Movement, 1961–1965

Source: Doug McAdam's "Tactical Innovation and the Pace of Insurgency."
© Infobase Learning

Another related question is what happens once a movement achieves what it wants to achieve. Some movements that achieve their goals simply dissipate and fade away; others choose new goals and continue their activism or become institutionalized as lobbying or nonprofit organizations. For instance, among the many movements that were part of the Civil Rights Movement were three strong organizations most widely recognized by their initials: NAACP (National Association for the Advancement of Colored People), SCLC (discussed above), and SNCC (the Student Nonviolent Coordinating Committee, which sponsored the Freedom Summer project discussed above). SNCC was instrumental in getting political support for legislation that barred racial discrimination and expanded blacks' access to voting and political participation in 1964 and 1965. But by 1967, the movement had begun to dissolve as members disagreed about what to focus on next, a process called **fragmentation**. SCLC is still active as an organization but has turned its attention to economic empowerment, health care, public education, and criminal justice issues. And the NAACP has become an institutionalized organization with many divisions and many employees and now concentrates on lobbying elected officials, monitoring and publicizing court cases related to issues of critical interest to the black community, and funding scholarships for minority students.

Some movements never do achieve their goals, either because all perceived by society as too extreme or because their strategies and tactics are ineffectual. Some may end by being co-opted by other movements. The Tea Party, for instance, began in 2009 as a movement of people frustrated by a government they saw as too big and too distant from their lives. By 2010, however, many political commentators came to believe that much of the Tea Party had been co-opted by the Republican Party, which aimed to use the popular support for the Tea Party to increase its own chances of electoral success. While Tea Party members are more likely to support Republicans than Democrats, the goals of the Tea Party are somewhat different from the goals of Republican Party. The most important priority of the Tea Party is to ensure that all proposed bills identify the part of the Constitution that empowers Congress to enact corresponding laws, while the most important issue on the Republican Party platform is national defense—an issue that does not even make the top ten list of Tea Party priorities. Other movements fade away because political opportunities shift. A classic example of this is the peace movement that fought against the Vietnam War as well as against the arms race that emerged during the Cold War. When the Vietnam War ended, many adherents of the movement simply dropped out. When the Soviet Union fell in 1991, the Cold War ended and thus another of the main targets of peace activists was removed. Smaller peace movements emerged during the 1990s when the United States participated in military actions in the territories that made up the former Yugoslavia, in Haiti, Liberia, Afghanistan, Sudan, and other countries. Peace activists also mobilized when the United States invaded Iraq, but the movement was largely absent from the scene for more than a decade—a period of **abeyance**.

Repression can also play a major role in ending movements. For example, elections in Iran in 2009 led to many allegations of irregularities in the voting process. When the election results were made public, people took to the streets to protest. Within days, as many as three million people were protesting, demanding changes in the political regime. But the government rapidly took repressive action against the protesters. Access to news, communications networks, and Websites was limited or shut off entirely; some protesters were killed; and hundreds of people, including opposition political figures and journalists, were detained or arrested. Many of those arrested were subjected to torture and some were executed. In the face of this repression, most supporters of the protests withdrew from the movement and it ceased to exist.

There are cases, however, where repression backfires and makes a movement stronger. Early in the Freedom Summer campaign, for instance, three activists were killed by white supremacists who were hoping that those deaths and the threat of future violence would discourage northern college students from coming to Mississippi to participate in the Civil Rights Movement; many other activists were beaten. This sort of violent repression causes some movements to fall apart, but the Freedom Summer activists were able to use it to their advantage. They trained participants in nonviolent resistance, teaching them to go limp and protect delicate body parts and to avoid lashing out against those who were beating them, even in self-defense. As a result, the national news media printed and broadcast images of nonviolent students being beaten by white supremacists, and these images increased support for the Civil Rights Movement. In fact, this had been part of the strategy of Freedom Summer all along: black activists had experienced violence without anyone noticing or caring, so they figured that getting some white students involved would finally make the rest of the country pay attention to what was happening in Mississippi and elsewhere in the South.

Not all repression involves violence. Activists may be subject to legal penalties, like imprisonment, fines, and criminal records. One example of such repression concerns an animal rights activist named Kevin Kjonass who protested in front of the homes of workers of a company that tests drugs, food products, and other chemicals on animals like dogs, monkeys, and rats, and then kills them at the end of the experiments. Kjonass and his fellow activists also engaged in some vandalism, like breaking windows and spray-painting "puppy killer" on one employee's property. He was ultimately sentenced to six years in prison for conspiracy under the Animal Enterprise Protection Act (AEPA), a law that turned damaging the business interests of companies that use animals into a kind of terrorism; six other activists in his organization were sentenced to shorter terms. Kevin and his six fellow activists became known as the SHAC 7 an acronym based on the name of their organization, Stop Huntingdon Animal

Cruelty. The AEPA and the sentencing of the SHAC 7 made many animal rights and environmental activists wary of engaging in similar assertive tactics. The Animal Liberation Front and the Earth Liberation Front, two groups whose activists have been targeted by the AEPA, now work mostly underground to try to avoid detection, and more mainstream animal rights groups have become reluctant to support them.

Violent or legally punitive forms of repression are common and obvious, but other repressive actions against social movements are more subtle. Tactics include fragmenting movements from within or using public opinion as a weapon. During the 1960s, for example, the largest student movement organization was called Students for a Democratic Society. The FBI had undercover agents infiltrate the group and place its members under surveillance; the undercover agents encouraged group members to engage in illegal activities and also worked to create dissention within the group, actions that helped lead to its end.

Discrediting movement participants can also weaken or even destroy a movement. During the 1950s, Senator Joseph McCarthy and other political figures spearheaded a movement to ferret out communists and communist sympathizers they perceived as threats to the United States. As the "Red Scare" grew, the House Un-American Activities Committee held hearings on the matter, targeting suspected communists or those who consorted with suspected communists. In each case, those questioned were pressured to divulge the names of other communists or communist sympathizers. Among those caught up in this process were many highly visible public figures, especially high-profile members of the film industry. As a result of these hearings, a number of actors, directors, and screenwriters were blacklisted from the industry, preventing them from working for many years.

A quite different example of discrediting involves anti-gay activists who argue that gay and lesbian people should be subjected to forced psychiatric intervention, that anti-discrimination and same-sex marriage laws should be repealed, and that gay and lesbian people should not be allowed to have contact with children (whether as teachers of other people's children or even with their own children). Gay rights groups and others have devised a means of discrediting the people engaged in such anti-gay rhetoric and activities by revealing that the activists themselves are engaging in same-sex sexual activity. While this might not seem to be a big deal, it is for individuals who have staked their careers and their activism on their claims to be able to "cure" people of their attraction to members of the same sex.

Activists can face much more mild repression as well, like disapproval or ridicule from friends and neighbors. Yet fear of repression, whether mild or severe, does not seem to be enough to stop millions of people around the world from creating or joining social movements and working to achieve a variety of different goals. One reason for this (and arguably the best reason for this) is that we inhabit a world that is imperfect, partly because access to power is unequal. Because these conditions are unlikely to change any time soon, social movements remain the best and sometimes the only way for ordinary people to try to create social change. The impacts of social movements range from the small and local to the major and global, but they have shaped all of our lives. Without the actions of social movements, women might not have earned the right to vote in American elections until decades later than 1920; blacks might still be restricted from holding political office in the South; factory workers (including children) might still be required to work 96 hours a week; and the release of many now-prohibited toxic chemicals into the environment might still be poisoning us (legally). As anthropologist Margaret Mead observed, we should "never doubt that a small group of thoughtful, committed people can change the world; indeed, it's the only thing that ever has." Social movements continue to underscore just how astute this observation was.

Further Reading

Amenta, Edwin, Drew Halfmann, and Michael P. Young. "The Strategies and Contexts of Social Movements: Political Mediation and the Impact of the Townsend Movement in California." *Mobilization.* 4:1–24, 1999.

Arthur, Mikaila Mariel Lemonik. *Student Activism and Curricular Change in Higher Education.* Surrey, UK: Ashgate Publishing, 2011.

Benford, Robert D., and David A. Snow. "Framing Processes and Social Movements: An Overview and Assessment." *Annual Review of Sociology.* 26:611–639, 2000.

Della Porta, Donatella, and Mario Diani. *Social Movements: An Introduction*, 2nd ed. Malden, Mass.: Wiley-Blackwell, 2006.

Ganz, Marshall. *Why David Sometimes Wins: Strategy, Leadership, and the California Agricultural Movement.* New York: Oxford University Press, 2009.

Goodwin, Jeff, and James M. Jasper, eds. *The Social Movements Reader: Cases and Concepts*, 2nd ed. Malden, Mass.: Blackwell Publishing, 2009.

McAdam, Doug. *Freedom Summer.* New York: Oxford University Press, 1988.

McAdam, Doug. "Tactical Innovation and the Pace of Black Insurgency." *American Sociological Review.* 48:735–754, 1983.

Meyer, David S. *The Politics of Protest: Social Movements in America.* New York: Oxford University Press, 2006.

Polleta, Francesca. *Freedom Is an Endless Meeting: Democracy in American Social Movements.* Chicago: University of Chicago Press, 2002.

Smelser, Neil. *Theory of Collective Behavior.* New York, Free Press, 1963.

Snow, David, and Sarah A. Soule. *A Primer on Social Movements.* New York: W.W. Norton & Company, 2009.

Walker, Edward T., Andrew W. Martin, and John D. McCarthy. "Confronting the State, the Corporation, and the Academy: The Influence of Institutional Targets on Social Movement Repertoires." *American Journal of Sociology.* 114:35–76, 2008.

CHAPTER 7

REVOLUTION AND REFORM

Some social movements are concerned with fairly small changes to the world—a new major at a college, the construction of a public park in an urban area, or the revision of a particular law. Others, however, seek much broader changes to society, changes that get at the fundamental organization of social and political life. But attempts to create such changes can come from other fronts besides social movements.

ELITE-LED SOCIAL CHANGE

In some circumstances, social change is spurred by members of the **elite**. In other words, those who have political, social, and/or economic power themselves orchestrate change. C. Wright Mills called the group that has the ability to create such change **the power elite**. The power elite is an interlocking group of leaders in military, corporate, and political life who use their power to maintain their interests. Similarly, in his book *Who Rules America?*, William Domhoff argues that the social upper class, corporate leaders, and policy leaders make up interlocking networks that work to maintain their power over United States politics and society.

The power elite's concern with maintaining its power and promoting its own interests means that in many cases its members oppose social change, preferring to maintain patterns and practices that have historically been beneficial to them. However, sometimes the elite does turn to creating social change that has benefits for others, particularly when the elite sees external threats to its power and control. For instance, during the Great Depression, the power elite supported some New Deal reforms. These reforms did not challenge the underlying nature of capitalist society but did provide social welfare benefits for the poor that had not previously been available. Many members of the elite looked with worry at communist revolutions in other parts of the world and realized that if they did not create reforms to forestall such revolutions, the deprivations of the Great Depression might lead to similar mass movements of the poor and unemployed in the United States that might overthrow elite power.

Many sociologists and other observers of society believe that recent changes in public education in the United States are examples of elite-led reform. For instance, many states and local school districts have experimented with **charter schools**—schools that are public and tuition-free, but exempt from many of the normal regulations governing public schools and run by agencies (such as private companies) outside the purview of local education departments. Politicians and reformers argue that charter schools are good for education because they provide alternatives to failing schools and allow educators to try out innovations that might improve academic performance. However, research on charter schools has shown that they are usually no better—and sometimes much worse—than regular public schools, despite often costing more to run. Yet there is still considerable support for charter schools across the United States. Why? Well, charter schools provide opportunities for for-profit and not-for-profit organizations to get involved in school management, sometimes with a chance to make money. They can undermine the power of teachers' unions and limit political control over what schools do. Sometimes charter schools are even used to encourage population changes in urban communities. For instance, fancy new schools that require high test scores or artistic skills and which are attractive to white middle- and upper-class families may be created to encourage such families to stay in the city, thus raising property values and pushing poorer families out of certain city neighborhoods.

REVOLUTIONS

Many attempts at creating social change go much, much further than the social movements or elite-led reform movements discussed above. We call these episodes **revolutions**. The term revolution refers to any rapid, significant, and far-reaching change in social, political, and/or economic life, which is why we call the Industrial Revolution and the Green Revolution revolutions despite the fact that they did not involve any mass mobilization directed at creating change. Scholars also talk about **revolutionary science**, or significant changes in how scientific knowledge understands the world. However, when we talk about revolutions as a form of social change, we tend to mean more specifically **political revolutions** or **social revolutions**.

Political revolutions occur when a state or government is overthrown by a popular movement in an irregular, extraconstitutional, and/or violent fashion and is replaced by a new state or government. In other words, political revolutions occur where people tumble an existing government by means that are not "politics as usual" and then create new ones to take their place. Thus, a recall election that removes a president from office or the assassination of a king by his nephew who then assumes the throne are not revolutions. The former is not a revolution because it relies on regular political mechanisms to change the government. The latter is called a **coup d'état** and is distinguished from a revolution in that the nephew who takes over and reconstructs the government was already a member of the old power elite. Coups d'états frequently occur when the military seizes control of a government.

Social revolutions are broader in scale than political revolutions. They still incorporate the overthrow and transformation of a government by a mass mobilization of the population, but in a social revolution this political change is accompanied by rapid and fundamental social, economic, and/or cultural change during or soon after the government is transformed. For example, the 1830 revolution in France removed King Charles X from the throne and replaced him with Louis Philippe and the July Monarchy. The July Monarchy was quite different from King Charles X's reign in political terms—Louis Philippe was constrained by the terms of a constitution, the number of people allowed to vote doubled, and the elected parliament gained much more legislative power. But these political changes did not extend to broader social change. Indeed, even the doubled electorate still represented only one percent of the French population! In comparison, consider the 1917 October Revolution in Russia. In February 1917, riots broke out that led to the abdication of the Russian monarch, Tsar Nicholas II, from the throne; he was replaced by an elite-led provisional government (and he and his family were assassinated a few months later). This short-lived provisional government was then overthrown in October by the Bolsheviks, who established a new government based on the principles of socialism. Thus, the October Revolution not only changed the government of Russia but also changed social and economic relations by redistributing land, nationalizing private businesses, seizing the assets of the Russian Orthodox Church, shortening working hours, and increasing wages, among other things.

Why Do Revolutions Occur?

When asking what factors cause revolutions to occur, we are really asking two different questions: first, under what circumstances revolutionary movements develop, and second, under what circumstances are they successful. Since there are many more revolutionary movements than there are successful revolutions, the first question is much easier to answer. Revolutionary movements develop when countries are faced with challenges or

Coups d'état and Revolutions in World History

People have been overthrowing governments for as long as governments have existed. Some governments are overthrown by mass mobilizations that develop into political or social revolutions, whereas others are overthrown by those who are already close to the centers of power, events that have come to be known as coups d'état. Consider this sampling:

Approximate Date	Country or Empire	Description
49–45 BCE	Rome	Julius Caesar marches on Rome, overthrows the government, and becomes the new dictator.
1368	China	Chinese peasants rebel against their Mongol rulers, leading to the establishment of the Ming Dynasty.
1688	England	King James II is overthrown by Parliament and a constitutional monarchy is established under William III.
1775–1783	United States	The thirteen British colonies establish their independence from Britain and become the United States of America.
1789	France	The first French revolution (followed by others in 1830 and 1848) overthrows the monarchy and establishes the First Republic.
1791–1804	Haiti	Toussaint Louverture leads a slave rebellion, establishing Haiti as the first free black republic.
1835–1836	Mexico	Settlers in Texas declare independence from Mexico; after a war, an independent Republic of Texas is established.
1850–1864	China	Peasants attempt to overthrown the feudal system but the rebellion is quashed by a combination of Chinese, French, and British forces.
1868	Spain	Queen Isabella II is deposed and replaced with a short-lived constitutional monarchy, followed by a republic.

difficulties that they are simply unable to deal with, given existing institutional and social arrangements. These difficulties may be produced internally, as when political leaders implement new policies that create massive unrest within the population and then do not have the capacity to respond to the unrest. Difficulties may also be externally produced, whether because of natural disasters, economic troubles, invasion by foreign powers, or global social change. In particular, revolutionary groups are likely to emerge

Approximate Date	Country or Empire	Description
1908	Turkey	Revolt against the reigning sultan does not succeed in overthrowing the monarchy but reinstitutes a parliament suspended since 1878.
1917	Russia	Russian monarchy is overthrown; later in the year, communist regime is established.
1918–1919	Germany	Monarchy overthrown and replaced with the Weimar Republic, a democratic regime.
1925–1927	Syria	Mass mobilization against French colonial rule in Syria. Although unsuccessful, it provided a model for later nationalist uprisings in the Arab world.
1949	China	Mao Zedong establishes the People's Republic of China. Opponents of communism establish the Republic of China on the island of Taiwan.
1959	Cuba	Fidel Castro and his supporters overthrow dictator Fulgencia Batista and establish a communist regime.
1960–1966	Congo	Riots lead to independence from Belgium and the establishment of a democratic republic, though the republic disintegrates into chaos shortly thereafter.
1979	Iran	Iran's monarchy is overthrown and replaced with an Islamic republic under Ayatollah Ruhollah Khomeini, the leader of the revolution.
1989	Czechoslovakia	A nonviolent general strike results in the end of communist rule.
2006	Nepal	Maoists revolt against the monarchy, ultimately stripping the king of his powers and establishing a secular, Maoist democracy.

in opposition to governments that are authoritarian, exclusionary, and weak. In addition to these background characteristics, revolutions tend to form only where there is some degree of economic deprivation and where a group of "professional" revolutionaries devoted to the cause exists. However, some analysts have argued that revolutions will become less likely in the contemporary world. They contend that the ever-extending reach of globalization, the changing configurations of geopolitical power with the demise of the

Soviet Union and the end of colonialism, the spread of formally democratic governments, or the increasing powers of surveillance and social control provided by modern technological developments are (individually or collectively) impediments to the kinds of revolutions that the world has seen in the past.

Because there are few successful revolutions, researchers are limited in their ability to demonstrate conclusively what enables revolutions to succeed. But some researchers have constructed careful comparisons to support arguments about the constellation of factors that can enable successful revolutions. Three of the most dominant explanations for successful revolutionary movements are the modernization hypothesis, the Marxist hypothesis, and the state-centered hypothesis.

The modernization hypothesis suggests that revolutions are likely to occur when there is a rapid transition from a premodern social structure, economy, and political system to a modern one. Such rapid transitions often create development lags that affect some parts of a country or some groups of citizens more than others. When such lags are substantial, social stress is high, social values no longer correspond with the social structure, and traditional social institutions are destroyed. Under these conditions, revolutionary movements will emerge to challenge the government. In this view, revolutionary movements will be successful when the government is too weak to repress them.

The Marxist hypothesis also focuses on a broad social transition, but to Marxists the truly important transition is the one between different modes of economic production. In particular, Marxists argue that the transition to capitalist production creates social strains and new types of economic oppression, thus generating a revolutionary movement. This movement is likely to be successful when the capitalist class generally is too weak to repress it. Some scholars have combined the modernization and Marxist hypotheses, arguing that revolutionary movements will be successful only when both the government and the capitalist class are weak.

Finally, the state-centered approach focuses on the configuration of government and international power. Where a country is peripheral to the world economy, where the government is repressive and disorganized, and where the government has power that is limited by geography or social arrangements, revolutionary movements are more likely to arise and more likely to succeed. Jeff Goodwin and Theda Skocpol are two of the best-known adherents of the state-centered hypothesis. They have argued that revolutionary movements are especially likely to succeed when they target governments run by personal dictators with strong connections to foreign powers or colonial administrations that have largely excluded local people from power (an arrangement called "direct rule"). Goodwin and Skocpol also posit that successful revolutions tend to mobilize elites and middle-class people (not just masses of ordinary people)—in situations where the elites maintain strong ties to the government, they are less likely to support a revolutionary movement and thus they provide a measure of protection for the existing government.

TERRORISM

According to the United States State Department, **terrorism** is the "the unlawful use of—or threatened use of—force or violence against individuals or property to coerce or intimidate governments or societies, often to achieve political, religious, or ideological objectives." This definition raises more questions than it answers. First of all, we can ask what the difference is between a terrorist movement and a revolutionary movement, or indeed between a terrorist movement and any social movement that uses violent tactics. To a great extent, the difference is in the eye of the beholder. A revolutionary movement that succeeds in overthrowing a repressive government is hailed as a liberating force; the members of a failed one are thrown in jail (or executed) as terrorists and traitors. Or, as the cliché goes, "One man's freedom fighter is another man's terrorist." If you are seeking the change, you see yourself as someone trying to start a just revolution. If you are the target of the change, you think of yourself as a victim of terrorism.

A sociological definition of terrorism is "the calculated use (or threat) of violence against civilians to further policy or ideological goals." Like the U.S. State Department definition, this definition maintains that to be considered terrorists, a group must use or threaten the use of violence against people and it must have clear goals related to the political sphere or other elements of ideology (such as religion). This means that violent actors who spread fear across a population for no particular reason, such as serial killers, are not terrorists. Neither are those who seek to change society but use only nonviolent tactics.

But how do we define actors who use violence against property but do not seek to harm people? Take for example the Animal Liberation Front (ALF), a group that seeks to liberate animals from mistreatment and harm, especially those animals who suffer from lab experiments. The ALF claims that its tactics include only actions that do not harm people or threaten their lives, but they do harass animal researchers, destroy property, and release animals from captivity. Because of their actions, the United States Department of Justice has classified the ALF under the rubric of "domestic terrorism," the same classification given to Timothy McVeigh and Terry Nichols after they bombed an Oklahoma City federal building and killed 168 people.

Another difference between the United States State Department's understanding of terrorism and the sociological understanding of terrorism is the sociological emphasis on *civilians* as the intended victims of terrorism. Of course, many revolutionary movements do harm civilians, particularly those associated with or supportive of regime being overthrown. Consider what occurred just prior to and during the American Revolution, when individuals supporting (or suspected of supporting) British colonial authority were often subjected to tar-and-feathers attacks. Stripped of their clothes and covered in tar (or another sticky substance, like molasses) and then feathers, they were paraded through town as traitors. The goal of tar-and-feather attacks was public humiliation, but in some cases victims were seriously injured—whether from exposure to the cold, injuries caused by the difficult process of removing the tar in a time before the invention of industrial solvents, or the fact that attackers sometimes used burning-hot tar.

Although such attacks are relatively common in revolutionary periods, most revolutionary movements concentrate their violence on individuals directly associated with the government. Here the State Department definition and the sociological understanding of terrorism part company. If only government officials are harmed—no matter how brutally—violence has not been directed at civilians and the episode would be unlikely to constitute terrorism under the sociological definition.

Finally, the sociological definition allows for a type of terrorism that is entirely excluded by the United States State Department definition: **state terrorism**. State terrorism refers to situations in which governments either explicitly spread terror through acts of violence and/or the threat of violence against civilians or provide support to nonstate groups that do so on behalf of those governments. According to the definition of terrorism advanced by the United States government (as well as definitions used by the United Nations and many other national governments), there is no such thing as state terrorism. The understanding here is that when governments create or sponsor terrorism, they do so within the bounds of their own legal power and that this must be considered "internal" affairs and thus such activities are not considered "terrorism." It is, however, clear that governments can and do spread fear and practice violence against civilians. In Argentina, for example, a government commission admitted that about 9,000 people were "disappeared" between 1976 and 1983, the years the country was under a military dictatorship. (Human rights groups claim this number could be as high as 30,000.) Some of the disappeared were opposition fighters; others were trade union members, students, and journalists suspected of being sympathetic to the opposition. From a sociological perspective, those who were "disappeared" were victims of state terrorism.

Terrorism can be carried out by groups or by individuals of all different types. There are both left-wing and right-wing terrorist organizations; terrorist organizations that are large and well-financed and those that are poor and disorganized; terrorist organizations in Westernized, developed countries as well as those in poor countries with barely functioning governments. Some people carry out terrorist attacks entirely on their own, without sponsorship or even advice from any organized terrorist group. One example of this kind of

A Taxonomy of Terrorism

		Type of Terror Act			
		Selective		Indiscriminate	
Terrorist Actor	**Government Sponsored**	*Domestic* ORDEN, El Salvador	*Transnational* "askari," Apartheid South Africa	*Domestic* Taliban	*Transnational* Hamas
	Not Government Sponsored	*Domestic* Army of G-d (AOG), U.S.	*Transnational* Provisional Irish Republican Army (pre-2005)	*Domestic* Continuity Irish Republican Army	*Transnational* al-Qaeda

Terrorist organizations can be distinguished from one another along three primary dimensions outlined in the table above. The organizations named in each table cell are examples of terrorist organizations fitting the dimensions of that cell.

First, we can ask if the terrorist organization is sponsored by a government (or if the terrorism is directly practiced by a government), or if it occurs outside government sponsorship.

Second, we can ask if the terrorist actions taken by the organization are selective—in other words, directed at specific targets related to the ideological or political goals of the organization—or if the terrorist actions are directed indiscriminately at the general population. For example, consider an imaginary terrorist organization opposed to modern technology. If this organization were engaged in selective terrorism, it might seek to blow up stores selling computers and assassinate computer programmers. If it were engaged in indiscriminate terrorism, it would seek to spread violence and fear throughout society rather than limiting its actions to target only those directly associated with technology. Of course, in reality most terrorist organizations practice both selective and indiscriminate terrorism; in the table above, they are classified according to the type of terror act that predominated during their activities.

Finally, we can ask if the terrorism is domestic in nature, in other words if the terrorist actors are attacking those within their own nation, or if it crosses international borders.

terrorist attack occurred in February 2010 when Andrew Joseph Stack III flew an airplane into an IRS building in Texas. Stack, who was protesting against U.S. financial institutions and arrangements in the United States, killed an IRS worker and injured 13 other people.

Though most terrorists are males between the ages of 16 and 40, terrorists can be male or female, of any age, race, religion, or background. However, there are some basic characteristics that terrorists tend to have in common, a constellation of factors called the **terrorist profile.** It is important to remember that some terrorists will have none of these characteristics and few will exhibit all of them. According to this profile, terrorists tend to be unemployed or otherwise socially alienated and they tend to have an inconspicuous appearance. Many have special skills that are useful in terrorist activities, such as making bombs, flying airplanes, or using communications equipment; as might be suggested by this fact, they are often more affluent and highly educated than others in their area. They have ideological sympathies to the cause for which they are acting, and most will have personal connections to other terrorists or to those who sympathize with terrorists. Most terrorists are biographically available (meaning they are unencumbered by children or jobs or other time-consuming responsibilities). Some researchers argue that terrorists tend to exhibit specific personality characteristics, like an ambivalent relationship to authority; recent research suggests that terrorists who engage in suicide bombings are likely to have been depressed or suicidal prior to becoming involved with a terrorist organization.

Terrorists use a wide variety of strategies and tactics as they pursue their political and ideological goals. These strategies and tactics are designed to maximize fear among the targeted groups and to maximize publicity about terrorists' aims, as well as to achieve specific goals (such as the assassination of opponents or the disruption of particular businesses). The weapons of choice for modern terrorists are suicide bombings, improvised explosives, or other explosive devices, but they also employ nonexplosive weapons like guns or toxic chemicals. Some people fear that future terrorists attacks will include nuclear weapons or biological weapons such as infectious diseases to kill people. If terrorists need money, they may resort to robbery, kidnapping, or sales of black-market goods to fund their operations. Terrorist organizations are frequently structured as small groups or "cells" that are isolated from one another so that one group does not know about others, thus reducing the risk of detection; members communicate by disposable cell phones, untraceable email accounts, and even couriers. Terrorist organizations also rely on media coverage to spread fear among the population, sometimes sending press releases to media in order to gain additional exposure. For instance, during the 2000s Osama bin Laden, then head of al-Qaeda, released several video and audio tapes designed both to communicate with his supporters and remind people elsewhere in the world that his organization was planning future attacks against them.

In recent years, particularly after the attacks on the United States on September 11, 2001, the world has become increasingly focused on terrorism. This has led some people to believe that terrorism is a new problem, but it is not. Indeed, the history of terrorism goes back thousands of years. Terrorists operated in ancient Judea (a large province governed by Rome that includes the area currently known as Israel), in 11th century Persia, in revolutionary France, in 19th century Russia, and during the Civil War era in the United States.

What is different about today's terrorism is that it has become a global threat rather than a localized threat, as well as the development of widespread fears about terrorism and related changes in social behavior and national policies. According to a recent Gallup poll, 42 percent of Americans were very or somewhat worried that they or someone in their family would be a victim of terrorism. Although the number of people responding this way has fluctuated

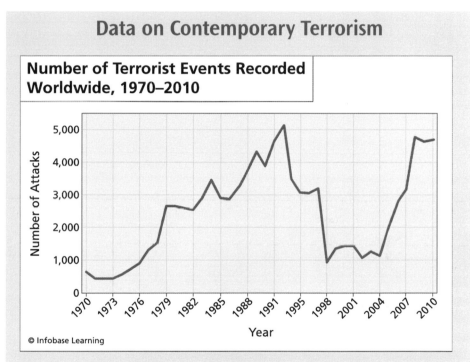

Data on Contemporary Terrorism

Number of Terrorist Events Recorded Worldwide, 1970–2010

© Infobase Learning

The data in the above graph include both successful and unsuccessful terrorist attacks, including those that injured or killed people as well as those that attempted property damage. Undoubtedly some attacks were not recorded.

The next figure shows that terrorist attacks are quite common in the Middle East, Africa, and South and Southeast Asia, but they are quite rare in East Asia, Central America, the Caribbean, Australia and the Pacific Islands, and Central Asia. North America is in an intermediate position, with 108 attacks between 2005 and 2008; of these, 72 were in the United States.

(continues)

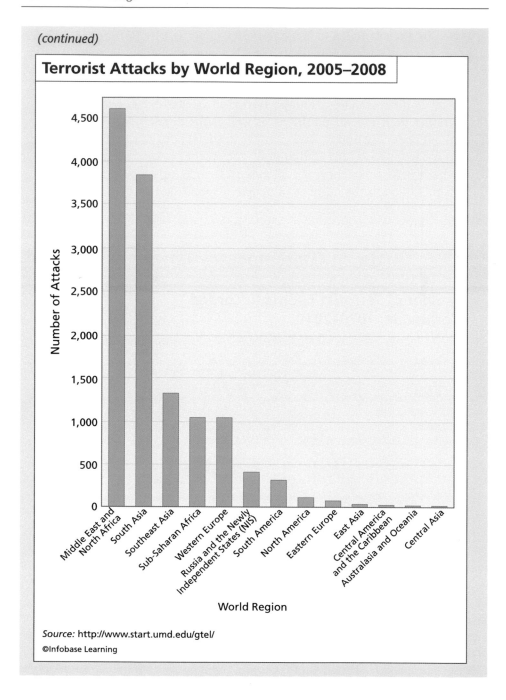

(continued)

Terrorist Attacks by World Region, 2005–2008

Source: http://www.start.umd.edu/gtel/

©Infobase Learning

over time, perceptions of the risk of terrorist attacks have been high at least since the Oklahoma City bombing in 1995. Many governments have channeled vast resources and numerous personnel to investigative and law enforcement activity related to terrorism. Their efforts include increasing surveillance of suspected terrorists and terrorist sympathizers, relaxing restrictions governing the detention and interrogation of suspected terrorists, and engaging in preemptive military strikes in areas were terrorists are believed to operate. Although some terrorism-detection methods, such as behavioral profiling of airport passengers, have been found to be quite effective, many remain controversial. It is always hard to tell what would have happened if a particular detection or law enforcement method were not in use, but at the same time many of the programs put in place to combat terrorism have invaded the privacy or violated the Constitutional rights of regular, law-abiding, nonterrorist citizens.

Terrorism, and even revolutions that do not use terrorism, are perhaps the most extreme actions that people can take in pursuit of social change. Those involved in these pursuits risk severe repercussions. Terrorists, revolutionaries, and even those just suspected of being terrorists or revolutionaries can be subjected to extremely harsh punishment, ranging from life sentences in solitary confinement to torture and death. In France, for example, anyone who ended up on the wrong side of a revolution was likely to face time in a dungeon and ultimately to have his or her head cut off by the guillotine. Richard Reid, known as the shoe bomber, was sentenced to life in prison without the possibility of parole, with his time to be served in a super maximum security prison in which his contact with other people is severely limited. Reid is not permitted to go outside or even see anything but sky, and his bed is made of poured concrete. For a time, he was even force-fed. In Iran, individuals accused of participation in any actions against the government—even peaceful street demonstrations—face torture and execution. Students in prison for protesting have been severely beaten, subjected to sleep deprivation, having their toenails pulled out, and raped.

Yet despite the possibility of such consequences, people continue to challenge even the most repressive governments and fight for social and political change. They do this because they believe deeply in their respective causes and because they know that if they don't fight for a better world, no one else will either. Though every human being in the world today has the chance to think about what would make the world a better place, and though every human being in the world today is forced to confront the consequences of all different kinds of social change, most of us will not have to confront the hard choices faced by the revolutionary—the very choices confronted by the founders of the United States. Imagine, for a moment, what their fate would have been had George Washington's army lost its battle with the British troops. Our history—and our understanding of who was a revolutionary and who a terrorist—would look quite different indeed.

Further Reading

Domhoff, G. William. *Who Rules America? Challenges to Corporate and Class Dominance.* Boston, Mass.: McGraw Hill, 2009.

Goodwin, Jeff. *No Other Way Out: States and Revolutionary Movements, 1945–1991.* Cambridge, UK: Cambridge University Press, 2001.

Kuhn, Thomas. *The Structure of Scientific Revolutions.* Chicago: University of Chicago Press, 1962.

Martin, Gus. *Understanding Terrorism: Challenges, Perspectives, and Issues*, 3rd edition. Thousand Oaks, Calif.: Sage Publications, 2010.

Mills, C. Wright. *The Power Elite.* New York: Oxford University Press, 2000.

Sanderson, Stephen K. *Revolutions: A Worldwide Introduction to Social and Political Contention with New Coverage of Terrorism.* Boulder, Colo.: Paradigm Publishers, 2005.

Skocpol, Theda. *States and Social Revolutions: A Comparative Analysis of France, Russia, and China.* Cambridge, UK: Cambridge University Press, 1979.

Vertigans, Stephen. *The Sociology of Terrorism: Peoples, Places, and Processes.* Oxford, UK: Routledge, 2011.

CHAPTER 8

RESPONDING TO SOCIAL CHANGE

Why did some people enthusiastically support the American Revolution, while others locked their doors and looked the other way and still others got involved on Britain's side? Why do some people excitedly buy all the newest technological gadgets while others use only what they have to and still others pine for the ways of yesteryear? A 2010 Pew Research Center poll found that 42 percent of those surveyed believed that U.S. population growth between now and 2050 would harm the country, 16 percent believed it would benefit the country, and 37 percent thought it would neither harm nor benefit the country. The remaining 5 percent had no opinion. Why do different people feel so differently about issues like this? Why is it that some of the people who think population growth will harm the United States keep this fear to themselves while others get involved in campaigns for zero population growth?

As the examples above illustrate, people can have extremely different responses to social phenomena, even people who live in the same country, share similar social and cultural norms, and are connected by similar or identical institutions. Some will go along, some will resist, and some will not care one way or another. There are differences even among those who see the need for social change. Some will keep their thoughts to themselves whereas others will become involved in efforts to create the desired changes. Chapter 6 discussed these efforts, which we call social movements, in more detail. Indeed, social movements can and do create social change. But they can also be a response to

Conflicting Opinions on Social Change in the 2000s

At the end of 2009, the Pew Research Center for the People and the Press conducted a survey to measure adults' opinions about the past decade. Among a variety of other questions, respondents were asked whether several specific social changes of the 2000s were generally changes for the better or changes for the worse. The graph below presents the results of this portion of the survey (respondents indicating that the change has not made much difference or who did not know are excluded from this graph).

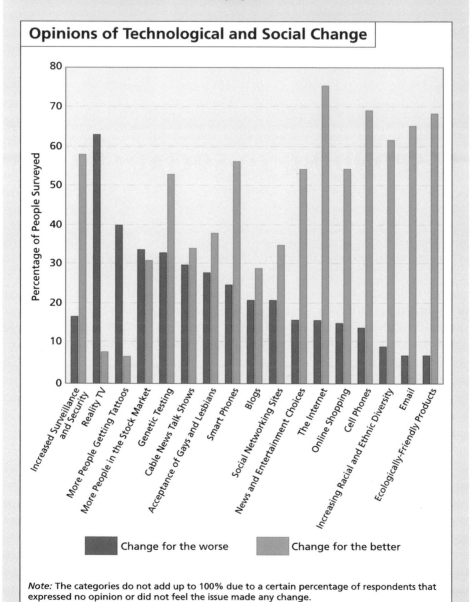

Opinions of Technological and Social Change

Change for the worse
Change for the better

Note: The categories do not add up to 100% due to a certain percentage of respondents that expressed no opinion or did not feel the issue made any change.

Source: 2009 Pew Research Center for the People and the Press Survey on Adults' Opinions.

social change: people get involved with movements because they are opposed to some direction in which society is going.

Sociology can tell us who feels what about social change. It can explain the dynamics of social change, in other words how and why social change happens. It can make predictions about what changes will endure and which will be overturned. It can tell us what the consequences and outcomes of various social changes have been and what they might be in the future. But sociology *cannot* tell us if any particular change—or social change in general—is desirable or undesirable, good or bad. Sociology is an **empirical** discipline, which means that it is focused on describing and analyzing those things that can actually be verified about social life. In contrast, questions about what is good or bad, what is right or wrong, or how things ought to be in the world are called **normative** questions. As discussed above, we all have opinions about the answers to normative questions—as we should. Each person reading this book will come away with their own conclusion about the relative advantages and disadvantages of each of the social changes discussed here. Sociology can provide us with the information and tools we need to help us develop opinions about social change, but it cannot tell us what we should think or what choices we should make about how to respond to social change.

RESPONDING TO SOCIAL CHANGE: CHOICES WE MAKE

Sociologist Robert Merton studied **deviance**, or actions that violate social norms. He came up with a typology which has come to be known as Merton's deviance typology and is designed to explain when people are likely to violate norms in specific ways. Merton's typology relies on two main concepts: first, the idea of cultural goals, and second, the idea of institutionalized means. Cultural goals are life goals that are generally agreed upon in society. For instance, in the United States, cultural goals might include making a lot of money, owning a house, and having children. Institutionalized means are practices or methods of achieving goals that are approved of in society and that people consider appropriate as ways to aspire to goals. For instance, getting a job is seen as a legitimate way to make money; robbing a bank is not. Merton's typology then classifies people according to whether they accept or reject cultural goals and institutionalized means. Those who accept both cultural goals and institutionalized means are *conformists*. Those who reject cultural goals but accept institutionalized means are *ritualists*. Ritualists might include people who go to work every day and do their job even though they don't want or need the money—these are the kind of people who die and it turns out that they had millions of dollars in the bank (or under the mattress) that no one knew about! Those who reject both the cultural goals and institutionalized means are *retreatists*. The conventional idea of the retreatist would be the hermit living alone in the woods. Conformists, ritualists, and retreatists are unlikely to produce social change.

However, there are two more groups in Merton's typology: *innovators* and *rebels*. Innovators are those who accept cultural goals, but reject the institutionalized means for achieving those goals. To Merton, criminals are innovators. For instance, the criminal who robs a bank to get a lot of money—or even the person who steals another family's child to bring it up as his or her own—would be accepting the cultural goals of money or children but finding new ways to go about achieving those goals. Innovators can do things that are not so criminal as well, and in doing so can sometimes produce social change. For instance, in many parts of the world, if someone owns property but does not take care of it and abandons it, squatters can try to move in and take over. After a given period of years, often seven to ten, and if the rightful owner has not tried to evict the squatters, the squatters get the rights to the property by adverse possession. In some areas, people have used this method to rehabilitate abandoned houses and ultimately rehabilitate dilapidated neighborhoods.

Rebels, in contrast, are those who not only reject accepted goals and institutionalized means, but move beyond them to develop new goals and new means. Rebels are the group most likely to create social change. Instead of seeking hom-

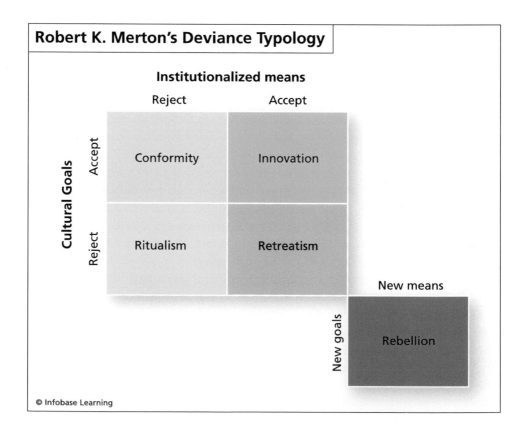

Robert K. Merton's Deviance Typology

Institutionalized means

Reject   Accept

Conformity   Innovation

Ritualism   Retreatism

New means

Rebellion

Cultural Goals — Accept / Reject

New goals

© Infobase Learning

eownership through making money, abandoning the idea of homeownership, or obtaining a home through adverse possession, a rebel might decide to fight for the abolition of private property by starting a social movement or a revolution. On a smaller scale, a rebel might decide to start a commune in which all property is held in common.

What Merton's typology tells us is that there are many ways of responding to social situations and that not everyone takes actions that might result in social change. Even when a group of people finds that the rules and institutions of society have made it impossible for them to live the life that they want, some people will just accept the situation as is, while others will take steps to find a new way of life. The same is true if we consider the ways that people respond to social change. George Ritzer, whom you may remember from the discussion of McDonaldization earlier in this book, outlines three responses to McDonaldization—and indeed to social change more broadly: *accepting, escape,* and *combating.*

People who accept social change fall into three categories: those who think that the world is better since the change, those who don't care one way or another, and those who do actually care, but think there is nothing they can do. Of course, almost all of us, except for the most committed retreatist, think that some forms of social change are good thing. Consider, for instance, the development of agriculture and the resulting social changes that allowed people to settle down in one place instead of hunting and gathering to survive or the invention of new medical treatments that prevent or cure common childhood diseases. When we believe that a particular social change has improved the world, we will accept that change or even work to further promote it.

People who don't care one way or another are those who are apathetic about the change. They might not think it is making the world a better place, but they don't think it is such a bad thing either. For them, the social change simply does not matter much to their day-to-day lives, so they ignore it. But some people think particular social changes are quite problematic and yet still accept them. These are people who feel that there is nothing they can do to make a difference. The discussion of social movements above would suggest that people often can make a difference, but in the moment—when someone is the only person they know who is troubled by something, or if someone has too little knowledge and too few resources to get involved, or especially if activism seems risky and hard to fit into life—they may not try to make a change.

On the other hand, some people who are opposed to particular social changes and yet feel they cannot make a difference still choose to do something rather than to accept the change as is. These individuals choose the option of escape. Escape is a catch-all term we can use for any way in which people seek to avoid the consequences or effects of some form of social change without doing anything to combat that change. There are many different kinds of escape. For instance, people who are unhappy with the political direction of the country in which they live may choose to leave the country and move elsewhere. Becoming a hermit, like the retreatists discussed above, is another alternative. Those who are opposed to new technologies or products like cell phones or Facebook might simply choose to cut themselves off from such technologies and products, and people can make similar choices with respect to news and other new information.

George Ritzer, in his writing on the McDonaldization phenomenon discussed in Chapter 3 of this volume, proposes an interesting twist on the notion of escape. He argues that there are some things in life which simply cannot be McDonaldized—specifically those things that are not predictable and not subject to control by technology. Weather is a prime example of this, and indeed Ritzer uses the example of climbing Mount Everest as one way that people pursue a less-McDonaldized existence. At the same time, he shows that just as people look to escape McDonaldization by pursuing unpredictable and uncontrollable experiences, they also seek to make them more predictable and controlled. For instance, today's climbers of Mount Everest have access to communications technology, weather forecasts, medications for altitude sickness, and a variety of other tools that make climbing the mountain safer and more predictable, and thus many more people are able to survive the climb. Climbers still die—at least five died on the mountain in 2009 alone—but compared to the 1920s, when many climbers died without getting near the summit, climbing Mount Everest today is much safer. A similar dynamic can be seen in many more mundane areas of life. For example, people seek an escape from predictability through gambling, but then learn to count cards so they can be assured of a higher winning percentage. Or they take a vacation to get away from work and find themselves checking in with the office continually. Thus, some attempts to respond to social change by seeking escape should not be taken too seriously.

On the other hand, escaping social change has much in common with combating social change. Individuals' choices about career paths and lifestyles can help individuals avoid the consequences of social change and simultaneously make an impact in combating it. For instance, someone running a small organic family farm may be able to live a more traditional lifestyle with little use of modern technology and can simultaneously make a difference in the environment, the local economy, and people's eating habits. However, such individuals are unlikely to escape social change entirely—for instance, the farmer may be subject to health inspections, and his or her business will certainly be impacted by the availability of cheap food flown in from around the world. On a smaller scale, individuals can combat social change by voting with their money. Choosing to buy traditionally produced or local goods

Luddites

Today, the term **luddite** is used to refer to anyone who is opposed to—and tries to avoid using—new technologies, particularly those that automate human tasks or involve computerization. A modern luddite might avoid using the Internet, self-checkout machines at the grocery store, and GPS technology in the car. But originally, the term luddite referred to members of a specific social movement. The movement got its name from a man named Ned Ludd who destroyed two knitting machines in England in 1779. Those participating in the Luddite movement were generally skilled textile workers in Britain. They believed that the mechanization of textile production would destroy their jobs and their way of life. Though sporadic activism had occurred as early as the 1600s, the Luddite movement really came into existence in 1811, when it began an organized campaign of smashing industrial machines. Such attacks became so commonplace that factory owners devised hiding places for themselves and their machines. In 1812 the British Parliament passed a law known as the Frame Breaking Act that made destroying industrial machinery a crime punishable by death. Although the original Luddites were an example of a group aiming to combat social change, today's neo-luddites can be best understood as a more generic group comprising individuals seeking to escape social change. Though anti-technology activists certainly do exist, there are few people out there in the world blowing up computers and destroying cell phone towers. Instead, people who are opposed to the social changes brought about by modern technology are more likely to just avoid that technology.

can make a difference in limiting the reach of industrialized and globalized production.

Individuals who have a strong desire to combat particular social changes are likely to become active in collective action. They will organize or become part of social movements or revolutions to fight for their own changes—whether that be a return to the ways things were before or the development of different social changes leading to what activists see as a new and better world. Indeed, it is important to remember that social movements and revolutions are phenomena that both initiate and respond to social change. Consider the social issue of abortion. Until 1973, when the Supreme Court decision *Roe v. Wade* made abortion legal throughout the United States, there had been little organized opposition to abortion. Indeed, those opposed to abortion already largely had what they wanted and it was those who were in favor of legalized abortion who were fighting for change. Once abortion became legal, the tables were turned. Pro-choice activists celebrated their victory, while anti-abortion groups became mobilized to fight against social change.

Tempered Radicals

This book has predominantly discussed social change as a large-scale phenomenon—as something that affects the whole world or entire nations. But social change can happen on a much smaller scale as well. Individual communities or even individual workplaces can experience social change. Debra Meyerson, a professor of business at Stanford University, developed the concept of **tempered radicals** to explain how people can make an impact and create social change at their own workplaces. Meyerson explains that tempered radicals are people who do their jobs well and are accepted in their work organizations but who nonetheless represent ideas that are not mainstream in the culture of these organizations. Rather than staging "organizational revolutions" (that would be likely to get them fired) or simply accepting the status quo, tempered radicals choose strategies like quiet resistance, finding opportunities, negotiation, and sometimes even collective action to change their workplace. Tempered radicals have had an important impact on many issues, like expanding hiring of people of color, providing spaces for nursing mothers to pump breast milk, or reducing resource usage. Although their initiatives might be limited to just one small workplace initially, they can spread to other workplaces—and ultimately they can result in much more widespread social change. The tempered radical framework is another reminder that anyone can make a difference in the world if they choose to make the effort.

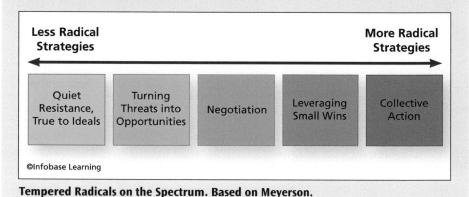

Less Radical Strategies ← → More Radical Strategies

| Quiet Resistance, True to Ideals | Turning Threats into Opportunities | Negotiation | Leveraging Small Wins | Collective Action |

©Infobase Learning

Tempered Radicals on the Spectrum. Based on Meyerson.

GOING FORWARD

The survey of social change in this book has been designed to accomplish two goals. The first goal was to introduce readers to the phenomenon of social change and thus promote an understanding of how our world got to be the way it is today and how change will continue to work in ways that will shape their lives. Learning about the development of modernity, the Industrial Revolution, globalization, and demographic change can help individuals to understand better the transition to the post-industrial economy, the continuing spread of global social and economic connections, the environmental challenges facing our world, and the impacts of continued population growth.

The second goal was to give readers an introduction to the tools necessary for creating social change themselves. The world is always changing, and—as this final chapter has shown—we can all choose whether or not to change with it and whether or not to fight for a different world. Everyone—whether well-educated or still in high school, whether well-paid or extremely poor, whether liberal or conservative—has opinions about the world, opinions about what would make the world a better place and what would make it a worse place, opinions about which social changes have been for the better and which have made things worse. By understanding how social change happens, and how individuals can play a significant role in making it happen, people can be better prepared to turn opinions into reality.

Think back to the very beginning of the book—to the story of disability rights that began with Carrie Buck being sterilized against her will and ended with the passage of the Americans with Disabilities Act. How does this story fit into a broader understanding of social change? The emergence of disability rights shows us how technological change can affect people's lives. It also shows us how a social movement can make a difference in the world. The story of disability rights also demonstrates how one social change can lead to another. As people with disabilities became integrated into public schools, the workplace, and the community, opinions began to change. That survey first conducted by the Minnesota Department of Public Welfare in 1962? It has been repeated periodically through the years, with the most recent wave in 2007. In 2007, only 15 percent of respondents thought that people with developmental disabilities are mentally ill, 3 percent thought those with developmental disabilities should be kept in institutions, and 2 percent thought they should not play in public playgrounds. People with disabilities still face stigma and discrimination in the United States, but clearly to a much smaller extent than they did five decades ago.

Changes like this came about because some people—individually and in groups—came to believe that there was something *wrong* with the way that those with disabilities were treated. Once that idea evolved, those people began to mobilize to make change. Not all social change happens because someone got the idea to make it happen. Indeed, large-scale changes like globalization, demographic change, and environmental change can happen because all kinds of insignificant individual decisions add up to make something bigger happen. But many types of social change happen because someone took the initiative. People invent new technologies and put them to use. They organize new types of neighborhoods, like Levittown, and new forms of social organization, like bureaucracy. They become involved in social movements and in revolutions. The study of social change shows us how very significant these actions can be.

In his book *The Eighteenth Brumaire of Louis Bonaparte*, a history of the aftermath of the French Revolution, Karl Marx wrote that people "make their own history, but they do not make it as they please; they do not make it under circumstances of their own choosing, but under circumstances existing already, given and transmitted from the past." The history of human society is thus not some automatic process in which the world progresses from point A to point B without any human intervention; nor can people simply choose to fashion the world according to their fancies. Rather, people make social change—and drive the engine of history—by navigating the complex circumstances in which they find themselves. These circumstances are the consequences of past social changes and shape future social changes, but they do not prevent change. People can always make the choice to make their world, or just their neighborhood, different from how they found it. The future is yours. What will you make of it?

Further Reading

Bornstein, David. *How to Change the World: Social Entrepreneurs and the Power of New Ideas*. New York: Oxford University Press, 2007.

Korgen, Kathleen Odell, Jonathan M. White, and Shelley K. White, eds. *Sociologists in Action: Sociology, Social Change, and Social Justice*. Thousand Oaks, Calif.: Pine Forge Press, 2011.

Kristof, Nicholas D., and Sheryl WuDunn. *Half the Sky: Turning Oppression into Opportunity for Women Worldwide*. New York: Vintage, 2010.

Loeb, Paul Rogat. *Soul of a Citizen: Living with Conviction in Challenging Times*, 2nd edition. New York: St. Martin's Griffin, 2010.

Merton, Robert K. *Social Theory and Social Structure*. New York: The Free Press, 1967.

Meyerson, Debra E. *Tempered Radicals: How Everyday Leaders Inspire Change at Work*. Cambridge, Mass.: Harvard Business School Press, 2003.

Piven, Frances Fox. *Challenging Authority: How Ordinary People Change America*. Lanham, Md.: Rowman & Littlefield, 2006.

Ritzer, George. *The McDonaldization of Society*. 5th ed. Thousand Oaks, Calif.: Pine Forge Press, 2008.

GLOSSARY

abeyance A temporary stop to something; the term abeyance is particularly used to refer to periods in which a social movement has stopped engaging in activism but could still reemerge in the future.

assembly line A method of manufacturing goods in which tasks are broken up and completed one at a time in succession by different workers or machines.

assertive tactics Social movement tactics that are designed to get noticed and to create disruption.

assimilative tactics Social movement tactics that are designed not to create disruption but rather to fit in with the way things are typically done.

bank run When a large number of people go to a bank all at once to withdraw their money, causing a high likelihood of bank failure.

biographical availability The condition of being available to do something, particularly to engage in social movement activism, because there are few or no obstacles in one's personal life (e.g., being single and without children).

birth rate The number of live births per 1,000 people per year.

blasé attitude Sociologist Georg Simmel's notion of a style of personal behavior in which even exciting and outrageous things are taken for granted or not even noticed.

bureaucracy A style of formal organization defined by a division of labor, a separation of jobs from job holders, a stable and hierarchical authority structure, rules and records that are maintained in writing, workers who need education and training, and action that is governed by rational thought.

capitalism   An economic system in which the means of production (land, machines, wealth, etc.) are privately owned; labor and resources are traded in markets; and profit goes to owners.

carrying capacity   The population size that an environment can sustain given existing land, food, water, and other resource levels.

charter schools   Public schools that receive public money but operate independently of regulations that typically govern traditional public schools.

city   A large, densely populated area.

collective action   Action taken by a large group of people all at once.

collective behavior   Actions taken by a large group of people all at once; typically seen as occurring spontaneously and not conforming to preexisting social norms.

collective goods   Services, products, or other goods that are equally available to an entire population no matter how many people are already consuming them, e.g. air.

commodification   The transformation of things into commodities, or goods and services that can be bought and sold for a price.

consensus   General agreement reached by a group as a whole.

countermovement   A social movement that arises in opposition to another social movement.

coup d'état   The sudden, illegal overthrow of a government by a small group of people who replace the preexisting government leadership.

credentialing   The process of establishing qualifications for professionals.

crowd   A large group of people.

cultural loss   When elements of a culture disappear, whether due to natural or social changes.

cultural structure   The patterns of ways of life in a particular society.

Dark Ages   The period following the decline of the Roman Empire and lasting until the European Renaissance and which was characterized by a cultural and economic decline.

death rate   The number of deaths per 1,000 people per year.

deforestation   A reduction in the land area occupied by forests due to the cutting down of trees.

deliberative process   A process of continuous discussion and communication until consensus is reached.

demographic transition   A period in which the death rate falls, leading to population increase, and then the birth rate falls, allowing population growth to stabilize.

demography   A social science field that studies human populations statistically.

desertification   A process in which land previously not desert becomes desert.

deviance   Acts that violate social norms.

diagnostic framing   Ways of explaining what a problem is and who is responsible for it.

diffusion   A process by which something spreads across a population.

divine right   The notion that a ruler has been placed in charge of a country by supernatural powers and is thus accountable to those powers rather than to the population at large.

division of labor   Splitting a work process among multiple people, with each worker specializing in a particular part of the process.

dot-com bubble   The period in the late 1990s in which the value of Internet stocks rose rapidly without being based on an actual increase in productivity or wealth, ultimately leading to a crash when the bottom fell out of the market.

early adopters   The first people to try something new.

economic capital   Wealth and other economic resources that someone owns.

economic system   The way that resources are produced, distributed, and consumed in a society.

elite   A relatively small group that has high and dominant status within society.

emigration rate   The number of people who leave a country per 1,000 residents per year.

empirical   Information that is obtained by way of observation, experiment, or other methods of verification rather than being based on opinions and values.

escape panic   A group rush to escape from a threatening situation, often resulting in injuries or deaths.

fad   Something that becomes very popular for a short period of time.

fashion   A style and custom popular at a given time.

fertility rate   The number of live births per 1,000 women of reproductive age.

feudal society   A society organized according to principles of feudalism.

feudalism   A system in which nobles owned land and ordinary people worked on the land with permission from the nobles; ordinary people owed work and military service to the nobles while nobles owed protection to the ordinary people.

flash mob   A large group of people that comes together suddenly and then leaves quickly, usually prompted to come and go via text messaging.

food riot   A group of people attacking places where food might be available because they are hungry or find that food prices have become too high.

fragmentation   When something disintegrates or falls to pieces; in the context of social movements, fragmentation refers to a movement falling apart.

framing   The construction of systems of interpretation to explain aspects of social life.

free market   An economic market in which government intervention is kept to an absolute minimum.

free rider   Someone benefiting from something that others worked to achieve without themselves participating in the process of that achievement.

fundamentalism   A belief in strict adherence to the rules and principles of some ideology or religion.

genetically modified organism (GMO)   A life form which has had its genetic material transformed through the use of genetic engineering.

Gini coefficient   A way of measuring economic inequality within a society by looking at the way income is distributed across the population.

global climate change   A significant change in world climate patterns; global climate change can refer both to natural changes like the Ice Age and to human-created changes like those currently occurring.

globalization   The process by which societies, economies, and nations around the world become integrated into a network of communication, trade, and cultural practices that spans the earth.

Green Revolution   A period in which agricultural production was transformed by the application of modern technologies, vastly increasing production.

grievances   A complaint about something that is wrong, which becomes the basis for action.

Gross Domestic Product (GDP)   The total value of all goods and services produced in a given nation in a given year.

herd behavior   Individuals in a group acting in concert, even without leadership or direction.

housing bubble   A sharp increase in the value of residential real estate that is not backed up by any objective change in conditions that would justify this increase.

immigration rate   The number of people who move into a country per 1,000 residents per year.

Industrial Revolution A period of technological change in the 18th and 19th centuries that resulted in the development of factory production and thus a significant increase in productivity.

industrialization The process by which industry (especially manufacturing) grows in extent and scale and becomes a more important aspect of the economy than agriculture.

infant mortality rate The number of deaths of children aged one or under per 1,000 live births per year.

information overload A state in which so much information is available that people become unable to process it.

knowledge industries Industries based on knowledge rather than production; examples are the media or education.

Late Capitalism An economic system that developed in the 20th century and is characterized by multinational corporations, globalized markets, and mass consumption of products.

life expectancy The number of years an individual can expect to live on average.

luddite An opponent of new technology; Luddite as a proper noun refers specifically to a movement of English workers in the 1800s who destroyed machinery because they opposed industrial production.

Malthusian catastrophe The theory that the human population would grow faster than agricultural production, leading humanity to face mass starvation before stabilizing at a much lower population size.

mania Extreme enthusiasm.

mass hysteria A condition in which a group of people all develop the same uncontrollable fear.

McDonaldization A process by which society takes on the characteristics of a fast-food restaurant, emphasizing rationality, calculability, predictability, and control.

McWorld A term used to describe the consequences of global McDonaldization on the world.

mechanization Replacing human or animal labor with machines.

metropolitan man Georg Simmel's model of how humans behave when they live in cities, characterized by neighbors who are all strangers to one another, relationships that are mediated by money, and a blasé attitude toward life.

mob A large, disorderly group of people.

modern society   Societies organized in accordance with the characteristics of modernity.

modernity   A period of human existence after the Renaissance, characterized by rapid change that is global in reach and extent and by the development of a new set of social institutions including the commodification of goods and labor, the rise of the nation-state, and the development of power sources that do not rely on humans or animals.

monocropping   The practice of growing a single crop in a given field repeatedly every growing season.

moral shock   A sudden emotional stimulus that causes an individual to realize that some aspect of social life conflicts with his or her deeply held moral views.

motivational framing   Ways of explaining a situation that encourage people to become involved.

nation-state   A country defined by the correspondence between its political structures and a particular national ethnic group.

network analysis   A method of data analysis that traces the connections between and influences of individuals or organizations that are part of a network of relationships.

normative   Statements that rely on norms, values, or morals rather than on evidence.

organic   Agriculture that does not rely on synthetic chemicals like fertilizers, pesticides, or antibiotics.

outsourcing   The transfer of business functions to organization outside of the business itself, especially when this transfer takes business functions to a different country.

overconsumption   A level of consumption of resources that has gone beyond what the natural environment will be able to sustain.

panic   Sudden fear that overcomes all other thoughts or emotions.

panopticon   An situation designed to make it possible to watch everything that happens without people knowing whether they are being watched; the term is based on a design for a circular prison with a guard tower in the center that was created by Jeremy Bentham in the late 1700s.

participatory democracy   A system for decision making in which every member of the group is able to make a contribution to the ultimate decision and which goes well beyond a simple majority vote.

peak oil   The point at which the maximum possible rate of oil extraction from Earth is reached, after which time oil production will begin to decline until no oil remains.

phonics A method of learning to read in which the connection between the sounds of spoken English and particular letters of the alphabet is emphasized.

political revolution What occurs when a mass movement topples a government and creates a new system of government in its place.

political structure The patterns of interactions and relationships between social institutions, especially in relation to the distribution of power in a society.

population pyramid A graph that shows the distribution of a population by age and sex.

postmodern society A society that is organized in accordance with the characteristics of postmodernity.

postmodernity The era of human existence that comes after modernity and is characterized by a rebellion against modernity, the development of Late Capitalism, and social fragmentation.

power elite C. Wright Mills's notion of a small group of people with interlocking power and influence in military, economic, and social spheres who control a disproportionate percentage of resources and exercise disproportionate influence over decision making in a society.

prehistory The period of human existence before the development of written language.

premodern society The period of human existence up until the Industrial Revolution and the development of modernity, premodern society is characterized by small-scale production, an agricultural economy, limited social variation, and small rural communities.

prison riot A collective revolt by prison inmates against prison administrators or guards, typically characterized by violence.

prognostic framing A set of explanations about what should be done in response to a problem.

race riot An act of collective violence resulting from hatred of one racial group by another.

rational choice theory A framework for understanding human behavior that argues that people make rational choices by weighing the costs and benefits of different courses of action and choosing the one that will enable the maximization of benefits and the minimization of costs.

rationality Reasoning based on logic and evidence rather than on emotion or tradition.

rationalization The process by which more and more of social life becomes governed by rationality, efficiency, and calculation rather than morality, emotions, or traditions.

reference group   The primary group to which individuals compare themselves.

Renaissance   A period of cultural rebirth in Europe that occurred between the 14th and 17th centuries.

repertoire   A group of potential tactics from which a social movement chooses what it will do; repertoires are defined by the time and place in which a social movement is active.

replacement rate   The fertility level that results in an exact balance of birth rates and death rates, thus maintaining a level population.

repression   Actions taken to put down or suppress something; in the context of social movements, repression involves actions taken to stop or prevent social movements from being active.

resource mobilization   A theory of social movements that argues that movements form when there is a sufficient level of resources to enable formation and that the level of resources that the movement has is an important predictor of movement outcomes.

revolution   A drastic and extensive change in some aspect of social life.

revolutionary science   A substantial change in the basic assumptions that underlie some field of scientific inquiry.

riot   Collective disorder that involves violence against people and/or property.

self-fulfilling prophecy   A prediction that causes itself to come true.

self-recruitment   When people mobilize themselves into a social movement without already knowing others who are part of it.

service industries   Industries that provide services to their customers, such as haircuts, medical care, food service, or house cleaning.

social change   Any change in the structures or practices of a society or social group.

social movement   An organized group of people without access to significant power who are working toward a goal.

social movement organization   A formal organization that is part of a social movement.

social network   A structure of individuals or organizations who are connected to one another.

social revolution   Something that occurs when a mass movement topples a government not only with the intent of building a new governing structure but also with the intent of instituting broader changes in economic and/or social life.

social structure   The patterns of relationships in a society.

sociology The study of society and social life.

sports riot Group violence and disorder in response to an athletic event.

state terrorism The use of violence and the infliction of fear by a government against all or part of its population, particularly when those targeted have not committed any crime.

strategic capacity The ability of a social movement to develop effective movement strategy; strategic capacity consists of motivation, access to knowledge, and leadership processes that enable the development of new ideas.

strategy An overall plan of action for achieving a goal.

sub-prime mortgage industry The industry that engages in the practice of making sub-prime mortgage loans in order to profit from them.

sub-prime mortgages Loans for the purpose of purchasing real estate, which are made to people who are likely to have difficulty repaying them; typically they have higher interest rates and/or fees than other loans.

suburb Residential area on the outskirts of a city that is characterized by lower population density with less industrial activity than found in cities and higher population density with less agricultural activity than are found in rural areas.

surveillance Monitoring the behavior or activities or people, often without their knowledge that they are being watched.

tactical innovation The development of new tactics by a social movement for the purpose of continued engagement in unexpected activities or to evade repression by the government.

tactics A particular action designed to achieve some goal.

target The particular focus of an action; in discussion of social movements, the target is the group, organization, or government that the movement is attempting to influence so that a change desired by the movement occurs.

Taylorism A theory of management in which work practices are analyzed with the goal of increasing efficiency and productivity.

technology Tools that help people think or act in ways that expand their capabilities.

tempered radical An individual who works to effect change within a particular social group or workplace by taking actions that are out of the norm but do not warrant being dismissed from the group or job.

terrorism The calculated use (or threat) of violence against civilians to further policy or ideological goals.

terrorist profile   A set of personal, social, and/or psychological characteristics that is supposed to help detect potential or actual terrorists.

totalitarianism   A system of government in which the government holds absolute control over the population and ordinary citizens have no authority or say in how their country is run.

urbanization   The process in which cities grow larger as more and more people move into cities.

viral marketing   A technique for marketing goods or services that encourages the spread of information about a product by word-of-mouth, especially by relying on Internet technologies to spread the message faster.

whole language   A philosophy of teaching language and reading in which recognition of words in context is emphasized.

witch hunt   A search for witches or the evidence of witchcraft characterized by mass hysteria but often involving legal forms of trial and punishment.

zero population growth   A term used to define the level of fertility needed to achieve a stable population level over time, as well as to reference a social movement that encourages such a level of fertility.

BIBLIOGRAPHY

Aguirre, B.E., E.L. Quarantelli, and Jorge L. Mendoza. "The Collective Behavior of Fads: The Characteristics, Effects, and Career of Streaking." *American Sociological Review.* 53:4, 569–584, 1988.

Amenta, Edwin, Drew Halfmann, and Michael P. Young. "The Strategies and Contexts of Social Movements: Political Mediation and the Impact of the Townsend Movement in California." *Mobilization.* 4:1–24, 1999.

American Sociological Association Website. http://www.asanet.org, 2010.

Anleu, Sharyn L. Roach. *Law and Social Change*, 2nd ed. London: Sage Publications, 2010.

Arthur, Mikaila Mariel Lemonik. *Student Activism and Curricular Change in Higher Education.* Surrey, UK: Ashgate Publishing, 2011.

Baldassare, Mark. *Trouble in Paradise: The Suburban Transformation in America.* New York: Columbia University Press, 1986.

Barber, Benjamin. *Jihad vs. McWorld.* New York: Random House, 1996.

Bauman, Zygmunt. *Modernity and Ambivalence.* Cambridge, UK: Polity Press, 1991.

Bell, Daniel. *The Coming of Post-Industrial Society.* New York: Harper Colophon Books, 1974.

Benford, Robert D., and David A. Snow. "Framing Processes and Social Movements: An Overview and Assessment." *Annual Review of Sociology.* 26:611–639, 2000.

Bennett, Michael, and David W. Teague, eds., *The Nature of Cities: Ecocriticism and Urban Environments.* Tuscon: The University of Arizona Press, 1999.

Bentham, Jeremy. *The Panopticon Writings.* London: Verso, 1995.

Berger, Peter L. *Invitation to Sociology: A Humanistic Perspective.* New York: Anchor, 1963.

Bjeljac-Babic, Ranka. "6,000 Languages: An Embattled Heritage." *The UNESCO Courier*, April 2000, 18–19.

Bornstein, David. *How to Change the World: Social Entrepreneurs and the Power of New Ideas.* New York: Oxford University Press, 2007.

Boyer, Paul S., and Stephen Nissenbaum. *Salem Possessed: The Social Origins of Witchcraft*. Cambridge, Mass.: Harvard University Press, 1974.

Caillods, Françoise, *et al.*, eds. *World Social Science Report 2010*. Paris: UNESCO Publishing, 2010.

Centers for Disease Control. National Vital Statistics System, *National Center for Health Statistics*. http://www.cdc.gov/nchs/nvss.htm (accessed August 22, 2010).

Central Intelligence Agency. *The World Factbook*. https://www.cia.gov/library/publications/the-world-factbook (accessed August 22, 2010).

Dash, Mike. *Tulipomania: The Story of the World's Most Coveted Flower and the Extraordinary Passions It Aroused*. London: Phoenix, 2010.

Della Porta, Donatella, and Mario Diani. *Social Movements: An Introduction*, 2nd ed. Malden, Mass.: Wiley-Blackwell, 2006.

Domhoff, G. William. *Who Rules America? Challenges to Corporate and Class Dominance*. Boston, Mass.: McGraw Hill, 2009.

Duhigg, Charles. "What Does Your Credit Card Company Know About You?" *The New York Times*, May 12, 2009, MM40.

Fleisher, Doris Zames, and Frieda Zames. *The Disability Rights Movement: From Charity to Confrontation*. Philadelphia, Pa.: Temple University Press, 2000.

Ganz, Marshall. *Why David Sometimes Wins: Strategy, Leadership, and the California Agricultural Movement*. New York: Oxford University Press, 2009.

Garber, Peter M. "Tulipmania." *The Journal of Political Economy*. 97: 535–560, 1989.

Giddens, Anthony. *The Consequences of Modernity*. Stanford, Calif.: Stanford University Press, 1990.

Gilbreth, Frank B., Jr., and Ernestine Gilbreth Carey. *Cheaper by the Dozen*. New York: HarperCollins Publishers, 2005.

Gilje, Paul A. *Rioting in America*. Bloomington, Ind.: Indiana University Press, 1996.

Goodwin, Jeff. *No Other Way Out: States and Revolutionary Movements, 1945–1991*. Cambridge, UK: Cambridge University Press, 2001.

Goodwin, Jeff, and James M. Jasper, eds. *The Social Movements Reader: Cases and Concepts*, 2nd ed. Malden, Mass.: Blackwell Publishing, 2009.

Goudie, Andrew. *The Human Impact on the Natural Environment*. Malden, Mass.: Blackwell Publishing, 2006.

Greenberg, Paul. "Tuna's End." *The New York Times Magazine*, MM28, June 22, 2010.

Hall, Stanley Granville. *Adolescence*. New York: D. Appleton and Company, 1904.

Harvey, David. *The Condition of Postmodernity*. Malden, Mass: Blackwell Publishing, 1990.

Hounshell, David A. *From the American System to Mass Production, 1800–1932: The Development of Manufacturing Technology in the United States*. Baltimore, Md.: Johns Hopkins University Press, 1984.

Imhoff, Daniel, ed. *Farming with the Wild*. Berkeley, Calif.: University of California Press, 2003.

Kanellos, Michael. "Perspective: Myths of Moore's Law." CNET News. http://news.cnet.com/Myths-of-Moores-Law/2010-1071_3-1014887.html (accessed July 11, 2010).

Korgen, Kathleen Odell, Jonathan M. White, and Shelley K. White, eds. *Sociologists in Action: Sociology, Social Change, and Social Justice*. Thousand Oaks, Calif.: Pine Forge Press, 2011.

Kristof, Nicholas D., and Sheryl WuDunn. *Half the Sky: Turning Oppression into Opportunity for Women Worldwide*. New York: Vintage, 2010.

Kuhn, Thomas. *The Structure of Scientific Revolutions*. Chicago: University of Chicago Press, 1962.

Loeb, Paul Rogat. *Soul of a Citizen: Living with Conviction in Challenging Times*, 2nd ed. New York: St. Martin's Griffin, 2010.

Lyon, David. *Surveillance Society: Monitoring Everyday Life*. Buckingham, UK: Open University Press, 2001.

Mackay, Charles. *Memoirs of Extraordinary Popular Delusions and the Madness of Crowds*, 2nd ed. London: Office of the National Illustrated Library, 1852. Available online at http://www.econlib.org/library/Mackay/macEx.html.

Malthus, Thomas. *An Essay on the Principle of Population*. London: J. Johnson, 1798. Library of Economics and Liberty. http://www.econlib.org/library/Malthus/malPop.html (accessed August 22, 2010).

Martin, Gus. *Understanding Terrorism: Challenges, Perspectives, and Issues*, 3rd ed. Thousand Oaks, Calif.: Sage Publications, 2010.

Marx, Karl, and Friedrich Engels. "Wage Labour and Capital." Marxists Internet Archive Library. http://www.marxists.org/archive/marx/works/1847/wage-labour/index.htm (accessed July 9, 2010).

McAdam, Doug. "Tactical Innovation and the Pace of Black Insurgency." *American Sociological Review*. 48:735–754, 1983.

_____. *Freedom Summer*. New York: Oxford University Press, 1988.

Merton, Robert K. *Social Theory and Social Structure*. New York: The Free Press, 1967.

Meyer, David S. *The Politics of Protest: Social Movements in America*. New York: Oxford University Press, 2006.

Meyerson, Debra E. *Tempered Radicals: How Everyday Leaders Inspire Change at Work*. Cambridge, Mass.: Harvard Business School Press, 2003.

Mills, C. Wright. *The Sociological Imagination*. New York: Oxford University Press, 1959.

_____. *The Power Elite*. New York: Oxford University Press, 2000.

Murphy, Elaine, and Dana Carr. "Powerful Partners: Adolescent Girls' Education and Delayed Childbearing." *Population Reference Bureau*. http://www.prb.org/pdf07/powerfulpartners.pdf (accessed August 22, 2010).

Noble, Trevor. *Social Theory and Social Change*. New York: St. Martin's Press, 2000.

Penenberg, Adam L. *Viral Loop: From Facebook to Twitter, How Today's Smartest Businesses Grow Themselves*. New York: Hyperion, 2009.

Piven, Frances Fox. *Challenging Authority: How Ordinary People Change America*. Lanham, Md.: Rowman & Littlefield, 2006.

Pollan, Michael. *The Omnivore's Dilemma*. New York: Penguin Group, 2006.

Polleta, Francesca. *Freedom Is an Endless Meeting: Democracy in American Social Movements*. Chicago: University of Chicago Press, 2002.

Ritzer, George. *The McDonaldization of Society*. 5th ed. Thousand Oaks, Calif.: Pine Forge Press, 2008.

_____. *Globalization: A Basic Text*. Malden, Mass.: Wiley Blackwell, 2010.

Rogers, Everett M. *Diffusion of Innovations*, 4th ed. New York: The Free Press, 1995.

Rowe, Peter G. *Making a Middle Landscape*. Cambridge, Mass.: The MIT Press, 1991.

Sanderson, Stephen K. *Revolutions: A Worldwide Introduction to Social and Political Contention with New Coverage of Terrorism*. Boulder, Colo.: Paradigm Publishers, 2005.

Simmel, Georg. "The Metropolis and Mental Life." In *The Sociology of Georg Simmel*, edited by Kurt H. Wolff, 409–424. New York: The Free Press, 1950.

_____. "The Stranger." In *The Sociology of Georg Simmel*, edited by Kurt H. Wolff, 402–408. New York: The Free Press, 1950.

Skocpol, Theda. *States and Social Revolutions: A Comparative Analysis of France, Russia, and China*. Cambridge, UK: Cambridge University Press, 1979.

Smelser, Neil. *Social Change in the Industrial Revolution: An Application of Theory to the British Cotton Industry*. Chicago: University of Chicago Press, 1959.

_____ . *Theory of Collective Behavior*. New York, Free Press, 1963.

Smith, Adam. An *Inquiry into the Nature and Causes of the Wealth of Nations*. London: Methuen & Co., 1904.

Smith, Alisa, and J.B. Mackinnon. *Plenty: Eating Locally on the 100 Mile Diet*. New York: Three Rivers Press, 2007.

Snow, David, and Sarah A. Soule. *A Primer on Social Movements*. New York: W.W. Norton & Company, 2009.

Stiglitz, Joseph E. *Globalization and its Discontents*. New York: W.W. Norton, 2003.

Stilgoe, John R. *Borderland: Origins of the American Suburb, 1820–1939*. New Haven, Conn.: Yale University Press, 1988.

Sztompka, Piotr. *The Sociology of Social Change*. Oxford, UK: Oxford University Press, 1993.

Taylor, Frederick W. *The Principles of Scientific Management*. New York: Norton, 1967.

Thompson, Clive. "What is I.B.M.'s Watson?" *New York Times*, June 14, 2010, MM30.

Timmerman, Kelsey. *Where am I Wearing? A Global Tour to the Countries, Factories, and People That Make Our Clothes*. Malden, Mass.: Wiley, 2008.

U.S. Census Bureau. "International Programs." *U.S. Census Bureau Population Division*. http://www.census.gov/ipc/www/ (accessed August 20, 2010).

Vertigans, Stephen. *The Sociology of Terrorism: Peoples, Places, and Processes*. Oxford, UK: Routledge, 2011.

Walker, Edward T., Andrew W. Martin, and John D. McCarthy. "Confronting the State, the Corporation, and the Academy: The Influence of Institutional Targets on Social Movement Repertoires." *American Journal of Sociology*. 114: 35–76, 2008.

Weber, Karl, ed. *Food, Inc*. New York: Public Affairs Books, 2009.

Weber, Max. "Bureaucracy," in *From Max Weber: Essays in Sociology*, edited by H.H. Gerth and C. Wright Mills, 196–244. London: Routledge, 1948.

Weeks, John R. *Population: An Introduction to Concepts and Issues*. Belmont, Calif.: Wadsworth Publishing, 2007.

Weinstein, Jay. *Social and Cultural Change: Social Science for a Dynamic World*, 2nd ed. Lanham, Md.: Rowman and Littlefield, 2005.

_____. *Social Change*, 3rd ed. Lanham, Md.: Rowman and Littlefield, 2010.

INDEX

Index note: Page numbers followed by *g* indicate glossary entries.